Dave Harvey draws on several decades of pastoral ministry, network leadership, and the teaching of the New Testament to coach us into a more collegial and fruitful way of leading—linking arms with other churches and watching the gospel surge forward more effectively than any single church could ever experience.

Dane Ortlund, senior pastor, Naperville Presbyterian Church, and author of *Gentle and Lowly*

Read carefully, examine yourself willingly, confess openly, and learn humbly because here is mature, gospel-rich, battle-formed ministry wisdom. In a season when the culture's individualism has tragically infected and weakened the church, this call to partnership in gospel ministry is an essential commitment that every pastor or leader needs to make.

Paul David Tripp, pastor and author of *Lead*

If we're blessed to see revival in our churches, I bet it will look a lot like the beautiful vision of partnership laid out by Dave Harvey. I encourage your church's leaders to work through this book together and trust God to develop a vision for growing stronger together.

Collin Hansen, vice president of content and editor-in-chief of The Gospel Coalition

As the leader of Acts 29, I am entirely convinced of the value of churches in partnership together, which is why I'm thrilled by the message of *Stronger Together*. This excellent resource is a model for choosing and thriving in church partnerships, and I commend this book to you.

Brian Howard, executive director, Acts 29

Stronger Together provides the rare opportunity to enter conversation with a seasoned leader who cares deeply about your calling and loves the gospel. Dave Harvey's words are wise, clear, and humble; they are biblically grounded and culturally astute. You will find empowering grace here.

Zack Eswine, pastor, Riverside Church, and
author of *Imperfect Pastor*

A timely and essential resource, *Stronger Together* gives you the heart and the strategy for starting and sustaining church networks. If you're a church leader—especially one who longs for a regional or city movement—this book is your go-to guide for humbly leading and stewarding church networks.

Daniel Yang, director, Church Multiplication Institute

This work from Dave Harvey provides a way for you to discover your position on the network matrix and to examine each quadrant's strengths and weaknesses. A book that celebrates virtue and warns against vices, *Stronger Together* will strengthen partnerships for kingdom advance across the country and around the world.

Trevin Wax, author, *The Thrill of Orthodoxy*

In this masterwork, Dave Harvey makes a clear and compelling case for the necessity and power of gospel-centered partnerships among churches for the advancement of God's kingdom. If you pray, "Your kingdom come," this book will help you better understand how God wants to use you to be part of his answer to that prayer.

Bob Lepine, teaching pastor, author *of Love Like You Mean It*, longtime cohost of *FamilyLife Today*

While many people long for unity in the church, Dave Harvey offers us a smartly written textbook on biblical collaboration. He speaks from years of experience as a network leader to offer us a field-tested guide for how to make networks work. If you believe that Jesus' prayer in John 17 was not just inspirational but also mission-critical, *read Stronger Together* and begin to live it out.

Dave Ferguson, lead pastor, Community Christian Church, and author of *B.L.E.S.S.*

God is honored by collaboration, and that's why I'm excited to recommend *Stronger Together.* Dave Harvey makes a strong biblical case for gospel partnership and collaboration, and he identifies the benefits of church partnerships and how networks can help the church produce more fruit. If you are passionate about Jesus and long to see greater impact on gospel outreach, read this book.

Patrick O'Connell, global director, NewThing

Grounded in Scripture and filled with examples and exercises, *Stronger Together* is essential reading for network leaders who want to lead more effectively, pastors who want to develop or deepen partnerships, and church members who want to understand how networks can strengthen church leaders and multiply church impact.

Dave Owens, executive director, Harbor Network

No one I know is better qualified to write a book about gospel partnership than Dave Harvey. Dave has experienced firsthand the incredible missional benefits of cooperation and the difficult challenges associated with Christian cooperation. *Stronger Together* offers a thoughtful, biblical, and balanced case for partnerships that every pastor should read.

Clint Clifton, founder, Praetorian Project, and author of *Church Planting Thresholds*

Dave Harvey provides a clear and compelling argument for the necessity of church planting networks to satisfy the Great Commission call. But he does so without diminishing the role of the local church. The wisdom displayed here will save many pastors and network leaders from falling into serious mistakes, including the growing tragedy of self-idolatry.

Zach Nelson, executive director, The Pillar Network

Dave Harvey writes with honest vulnerability and gospel centrality. *Stronger Together* will lead you toward an interdependent team approach in ministry. We all want that, but our self-serving habits are hard to break. I couldn't put the book down because of my passion for this kind of partnership in the gospel.

Scott Thomas, executive pastor of church multiplication, Immanuel Nashville, and author of *The Gospel-Shaped Leader*

Striking a perfect balance between the practical and the ideal, Dave Harvey offers us a vision for collaboration that is rooted in Scripture and that reaches for the blue sky of the kingdom. This is the conversation and these are the tools we most need for the future of the church.

Brian Sanders, founder, Underground Network, and author of *Underground Church*

Stronger Together is an exceptional work on the partnership of churches in multiplication. I appreciated the virtue-vice structure of the book, which made it easy to digest and apply. Everyone interested in or actively involved in church planting should read this book as a resource for ensuring that our collaborations are healthy and helpful.

Clayton Greene, director, Summit Collaborative

Dave Harvey has gifted us with a humility-nurturing, Christ-accentuating, strengthening work for church and network leaders and pastors. His personal journey brings a gospel-soaked wisdom and a compelling vision for the issue of why churches are "stronger together" in following Christ in his Great Commission.

Sean Cordell, executive director, Treasuring Christ
Together church planting network

Stronger Together makes a compelling biblical case for the necessity of collaborative gospel partnerships in the fulfillment of the Great Commission. This book is clearly the fruit of many years in the cauldron of learning and losses that produce practical wisdom. I'm grateful for Dave Harvey's humble and helpful counsel that prompts us to create strong, healthy networks for gospel saturation.

Jeff Vanderstelt, founding leader of Saturate
and the Soma Family of Churches and author
of *Gospel Fluency*

Rarely will you find a book whose questions leave you reflecting for days on end, where the applications are so practical you can apply them immediately and the principles so clear that you find your biblical conviction renewed and passion reinvigorated. *Stronger Together* is one of those rare books.

Dhati Lewis, founder and president, MyBLVD,
and lead pastor, Blueprint Church

Partnerships plant churches! I loved reading *Stronger Together* and being reminded that our mission as a church is more effective when we work together. If your heart beats for churches that are stronger together, you'll want to read this book.

Chad Clarkson, executive director, Houston Church
Planting Network

Collaboration is a necessity for the fulfillment and completion of the Great Commission. Dave Harvey does a brilliant job reminding us that the mission is larger than any one church, network, or denomination. If we long to see true kingdom movement happen, relational networks outside of our tribe will be needed to ignite the fire. *Stronger Together* will help light the match.

Will Plitt, executive director, Christ Together

STRONGER
TOGETHER

STRONGER TOGETHER

7 PARTNERSHIP VIRTUES and the VICES THAT SUBVERT THEM

DAVE HARVEY

ZONDERVAN REFLECTIVE

Stronger Together
Copyright © 2023 by Dave Harvey

Requests for information should be addressed to:
Zondervan, *3900 Sparks Dr. SE, Grand Rapids, Michigan 49546*

Zondervan titles may be purchased in bulk for educational, business, fundrais-ing, or sales promotional use. For information, please email SpecialMarkets@ Zondervan.com.

ISBN 978-0-310-14022-1 (softcover)
ISBN 978-0-310-14024-5 (audio)
ISBN 978-0-310-14023-8 (ebook)

Cover design: Studio Gearbox
Cover photo: © AntonPix / Shutterstock
Interior design: Kait Lamphere

Printed in the United States of America

23 24 25 26 27 28 29 30 31 /TRM/ 13 12 11 10 9 8 7 6 5 4 3 2 1

To *the planters and pastors of*
Great Commission Collective—

Because the gospel is so worthy,
it's glorious to even make the attempt.

CONTENTS

Part 4: The Character of Partnership

INTRODUCTION

When Pastors Need More Than Each Other

Twenty-five years. It's been a while, but I'll never forget the twenty-fifth anniversary celebration in the church where I pastored. To commemorate, our leadership and a team of volunteers transformed a portion of our church building into a gallery of memories—a museum that would remind the congregation of God's faithfulness through our journey together.

When we thought about how to mark the moment, one of our pastors had an idea: "Let's make certain the exhibit reflects the church's diversity by inviting a cross section of our members to share their experience of the church." That pastor gathered singles, parents, children, newlyweds, those who had just joined, and those who had been there for the whole ride. Each person was assigned a section of the museum where they could portray what they experienced and treasured about our church's history. An eleven-year-old was given a space and told, "This is your wall. Go. *Create!*"

Then one evening, right before the anniversary day, the ribbon was cut, and a small group who had been there from the first five years entered the museum. We approached slowly, wondering how twenty-five years of history would be remembered, how it would be portrayed.

Turning the corner, this is what I saw.

There were seven exhibits spaced throughout the room. Each one was a visual depiction of the church's ministry and values—outreach, children's ministry, youth, community life. Turning to my right, I saw a beautiful memorial wall to members we had lost.

But perhaps the most surprising, the most striking, of displays was the wall dedicated to our long-standing partnership with our church planting network. The display included copies of magazines, T-shirts from events, and even pictures of leaders who had visited our church as guest speakers. On the wall there was a space dedicated to the churches we had helped to plant— eleven new churches over two and a half decades.

Spread across the length of the exhibit hall was a two-hundred-foot banner—a timeline that captured important moments from the church's history. A quick glance at those events illustrated the seamless connection between our local church and our network partnership. It would have seemed impossible to separate the two organizations' histories.

As I stood and pondered the display, I remembered something. What I beheld was not a version of our history intentionally manufactured by a paid staff member. No, this wall reflected the *vision of church members*. It was their interpretation of essential influences that had shaped what our church had become, our identity. It was their history to tell. And when they told it, our church planting network was a vital part of the story. The people saw that when it came to our journey over the last twenty-five years, this partnership made an enduring difference. We were stronger together.

Pluralities Need Partnerships

Maybe your church has never been a part of a network or denominational partnership and you can't relate to my story. Or maybe you've been there, done that, and have left underwhelmed by the experience. Perhaps you long for connection and have a dream for your own twenty-five- or fifty-year anniversary. You want to plant churches. You want to serve fruitfully. You want to finish strong. Or maybe you have questions. Good questions like:

- Where should my church go to find a place where we can feel connected to God's larger mission?
- How can we learn to become a healthy elder team that endures over time? And where do we turn for help when the leadership team gets messy?
- If we want to start a new church, how do we find and train potential church planters? Then how do we support them so they can flourish?
- What does it look like for us to care for each other? Or care for a lead pastor? Where do elders learn this stuff?
- Where can we find collaboration that will stir our faith and kick-start our thinking about how to grow our church?
- We've got a group of churches that want to form a network. Where can we turn to find help in launching it?

Questions like these shadow me. It's not their complexity but their frequency. You don't need to lead a church for very long before you discover that not all needs can be resolved through more leaders meetings. Sometimes, in fact, the elders may be the problem—their lack of training or their misalignment.

Other times, it may be that the elders are longing to move forward on mission, but the lead pastor is building a platform, not a ministry team.

Yep, questions like these have kept me up at night. When you spend most of your adult life helping pastors and church leadership teams, this stuff gets stitched into your bones. And I'm not a remote observer of ministry and mission drama. I've been a senior pastor and a network leader. I've helped church plants that no longer exist and wondered what more I could have done. Mistakes? I've made plenty. And yes, there were times when ministry brought misery. Yet through the dangers, toils, and snares, I can testify that an essential means of grace for every church I've been a part of has been our vital link to an outside partnership.

Churches are planted and built because of the vital connections between churches—because of the mission they share together in a partnership. My experience of network—with all of its virtues and vices—has confirmed this biblical principle: *churches can achieve together what no one church could accomplish alone.*

Churches can achieve together what no one church could accomplish alone.

Being part of a network was a grace for our church when I served as a senior pastor. Overall, I was in that network for more than thirty years. Since that time, I've served in other churches from various traditions. I've also held different church network roles—first as an interim president of a group that had plummeted into organizational crisis, then as the president of two different church planting networks. I've seen churches tilt inward, fortify their independence, and check connection at the church's borders. But I've also watched in awe as partnerships lifted leaders and churches to greater gospel fruitfulness.

Just to be clear, I'm a local church guy, which means I see

networks as supplemental blessings. I believe they should never displace the responsibilities of local church leadership. My last book, *The Plurality Principle*, was dedicated to helping local church leaders understand the indispensable importance of a finely tuned elder plurality.[1] If you don't have solid convictions or clarity about the priority of the local church and how to do ministry as an elder team, set this book aside immediately and pick up the other book.

But healthy plurality was never intended to be the whole picture.

We know it's not good for man to be alone (Genesis 2:18). And we know leaders thrive best in the context of a team. But what if the needs and opportunities for local church leaders are greater than what can be met internally? What if it's not good for a church to be alone?

Local churches not only need elder teams, but they also need what Paul calls "partnership in the gospel" (Philippians 1:5). Interdependence, both locally and through extra-local affiliations (denominations, networks, and parachurch partners), completes the circle of influence to maximize our strengths and bring aid to our weaknesses. Just as people wither and perish in isolation, so does the local church.

Paul labored tirelessly to keep churches informed and connected. He deployed his helpers to the same ends. Paul not only argued that church members are indispensably related to one another (1 Corinthians 12:12–18), but he also believed that churches cannot be totally independent entities. Not if they want to remain resilient. Not if they want leaders who last. Not if they want to see the mission expand through planting renewable churches.

Through study and experiences, I'm now even more convinced that the biblical call to interdependence is not fully satisfied by merely connecting leaders and people together in the same local church. That's essential, but there's more. When churches are vitally connected to other churches, they thrive, multiply, and last longer. Or to return to our partnership principle: *churches can achieve together what no one church could accomplish alone.*

Networks Need to Pursue Health

Following Paul's model, networked churches today have become a formidable force in North American missions (and in many places abroad). Begun organically, these movements have become catalytic instruments for God's mission. In fact, networks and collectives are the primary church planting force in evangelicalism today.

But church planting networks only remain effective in accomplishing their mission to the degree they play to their strengths and avoid common weaknesses. Over my time serving networks, I've seen some ugly times when a network's noble goals got lost and baser instincts began to determine the course. When I think back over my history, it grieves me to say I've contributed my fair share to network problems. Now I pray regularly that God will help me labor to supply solutions. As for where this adventure has left me, well, to this very day I'm still embedded in the glorious chaos of network leadership, working daily to help church leaders plant strong and last long.

Over the trial-and-error pathway of my partnership adventures, I've searched the Scriptures and sat across from people much smarter than me. Through study and conversation, I've discovered seven key virtues that help networks thrive. And when these virtues are lost, vices grow—opposing forces that threaten network momentum and fruitfulness. If we are serious about building healthy, multiplying networks, we must wage war against these powers. To that end, this book focuses on seven polarities:

1. Conviction against consumerism
2. Gifted leadership against isolationism
3. Collaboration against radical individualism
4. Renewal dynamics against institutionalism
5. A kingdom mindset against tribalism
6. Humility against egotism
7. Modesty against triumphalism

As we explore these virtues and vices, my prayer is that we will be filled with fresh urgency to plant churches and start networks. I pray that you'll believe the truth and then experience the reality that *churches can achieve together what no one church could accomplish alone.*

Think about it. What if local churches are made stronger by their exposure to the grace of God in other local churches? What if the principle of interdependence is intended to apply beyond believers to local churches? What if the mission to which we are called was designed to flow through the unity to which we are pledged in partnerships?

Stronger Together

Allow me to be clear. This book is not about the benefits of ecumenism. That may be a worthy goal for a different author, but my intent is sharper, more targeted. In these pages, I will describe the virtues that help church planting networks thrive.

We will discover together as we examine the New Testament that interdependence was experienced at every level of church life—among members, within elderships, and between churches.

Partnerships are not only biblical, but they are also essential for planting churches and sustaining leaders in a fragmented world.

These are perilous times for planters and pastors. Suspicion of the church is high, pastoral credibility is low, and leaders are made dizzy by increasingly complex and polarizing pastoral issues. Pastors lack motivation for the mission and often serve daily under a cloud of loneliness.

When the world, the flesh, and the enemy are working overtime to suck their souls dry, to whom can leaders turn for help? When elderships are locked in conflict, where do they find clarity, support, and safe harbor? When they're unable to organize well enough to fulfill their dreams for church planting, where do they find a mission catalyst? When a church is experiencing mission drift, where can it find help to recover its vision?

I believe partnerships—*churches networked together for multiplication through message, ministries, models, movement, and money*—is the answer.

Deep into my fourth decade of ministry, I'm devoting the rest of my life to helping leaders and churches find solutions. I want to see the next generation of network leaders understand the possibilities and perils of church planting movements. I long to see churches flourish in community, thrive through church planting, and persevere beyond one generation. I'm more convinced than ever that partnership is a crucial piece in the puzzle of leader longevity and mission impact.

The time to plant churches is now. The time to disciple the next generation of planters is now. The time to build a multiplying church is now. The time to invest in partnership virtues and fight against the vices . . . is now.

This work is worth it, because *churches can achieve together what no one church could accomplish alone*. Now more than ever, we are stronger together.

PART
1

FOUNDATIONS FOR PARTNERSHIP

VIRTUE

CONVICTION

Against Consumerism

Daryl leads a small rural church. He has two lay elders who serve the church tirelessly. They love their church, but they are longing to connect the people to something bigger. They want the congregation to play their part in the Great Commission. These elders know that the church will be nourished by participating in God's mission locally, nationally, and globally. One evening while hanging out around a fire, Daryl asked the other men, "Where can we find a place to feel connected that also allows us to be a part of the larger mission?"

The elders at Elmwood Church have a man who is ready to be a church planter—or at least they hope they do. But they're nervous. Elmwood has never planted a church before, and the leadership team feels clueless about where to start. After a lengthy conversation during last week's elders meeting, the board chair summarized their discussion: "We need to find some folks who can help us evaluate and train our candidate and then advise us on how to actually plant the church. Where do we begin?"

John has been a lead pastor for ten years. The church John pastors is located close to a seminary, and he's drawn a crowd of young leaders. John is also part of a group of area pastors who gather regularly to pray and collaborate for the sake of reaching their city. Recently, after considerable prayer, an idea was born: *Let's form a network to plant churches in the metroplex.* John loved the idea and agreed to lead the team to help define their vision, their goals, and the nature of their alignment. Where can this group of churches turn to find help in launching a network?

W here do church leaders turn when they are confronted with knotty problems that seem beyond their experience and expertise? Where do they go when they are impaled on a prickly pastoral dilemma or stalled in their efforts to move forward?

In those times, it is the presence of *partnerships*—entities outside a local church—that helps move the mission forward. Often the role of a partner is *formal*; it's an affiliation with a church planting network. But at other times, the relationship is *less formal*. Leaders call an adviser, trusted friend, consultant, or counselor for help. On each of these occasions, indispensable help can come from outside a local church's eldership—actually from outside the local church.

For most of the world, this is a no-brainer. If a business hits a wall, qualified consultants are a phone call away. Good companies hire strong talent and then, where needed, outsource. Ironically, they sometimes downsize the good talent and then rehire them as consultants. In the marketplace, subbing out projects or problems is part of the business plan. Partnerships are formed, and mergers are forged. Collaboration gets radical when it's driven by profit and return on investment (ROI).

But that's not the kind of partnership I'm writing about. When it comes to biblical partnerships, something more than pragmatics and ROI must be in view.

Behold the Virtue:
Great Commission Conviction

Ron was a gifted pastor who led a large church. He was interested in joining our network, but he wondered aloud about whether it really had value for his church: "Will we really benefit from the partnership?" It was a reasonable question. For a partnership to make sense, there must be the promise of meaningful results. Questions over stewardship, after all, are the necessary responsibility of wise pastors.

"Ron," I said, "you're asking good questions. But don't let those good questions obscure a more important one."

Ron stopped and paused thoughtfully. "What's the more important question?"

"It's this," I answered. "Do you believe churches are stronger together? Do you believe church partnership is the clear testimony of the Bible?"

Suddenly our discussion shifted from felt needs to biblical practice, and Ron began to see a higher principle at play. Commitments to church partnership must be rooted in something greater than consumerism and market demands; they must be rooted in biblical doctrine and clear-eyed conviction. To thrive, churches in a partnership must believe that their efforts find their origin in God's design. They must be able to point to reasons for their partnership in the pages of Scripture. To flourish, partnerships must be grounded in biblical conviction.

To thrive, churches in a partnership must believe their efforts find their origin in God's design.

Partnership is so fundamental to New Testament missions that it's embedded in the Great Commission:

Now the eleven disciples went to Galilee, to the mountain to which Jesus had directed them. And when they saw him they worshiped him, but some doubted. And Jesus came and said to them, "All authority in heaven and on earth has been given to me. Go therefore and make disciples of all nations, baptizing them in the name of the Father and of the Son and of the Holy Spirit, teaching them to observe all that I have commanded you. And behold, I am with you always, to the end of the age." (Matthew 28:16–20)

Let me ask you a question. To whom was this commission directed? The eleven disciples were certainly in view; they were the original audience of Jesus' words. But Matthew's audience wasn't confined to the Eleven alone. The scope of Jesus' command expands geographically ("go therefore and make disciples of all nations"), and its duration goes well beyond the lifespan of those first disciples ("to the end of the age"). You see, the Eleven received the Great Commission as representatives. But who and what were they representing?

The Who: The Eleven represented the church. The Eleven (soon to return to the Twelve!) were used in a historically unique way to inaugurate the church, to formulate and develop its faith and doctrine, and to catalyze gospel expansion. By the Spirit's power and through the work of the Twelve, the church was born, nurtured, and began to multiply.

But the Great Commission doesn't stop with them; it still makes a claim on individual Christians today. No believer is exempt. As John Piper writes, "[The Great Commission] was not only given to the apostles for their ministry but also to the church for its ministry as long as this age lasts."[1]

Here's my point. When asking, "Who is the audience for the Great Commission?" the Eleven received it; the church will finish it.

The What: The Eleven represented a compass for missions.
A good compass helps us locate where we are and then points us forward. It helps us move in the right direction. The Great Commission was given to the apostles, but the way they applied it becomes a pattern for how missions would be led in the New Testament age. "The primary historical significance of the Great Commission," says missiologist George Peters, "lies in the fact that it gives to the church the pattern and purpose of missions. It defines and delineates the missionary task. We have in the Great Commission a compass, a charter, and a plan."[2]

This pattern and plan for missionary leadership not only started with the church but continued through Paul and his helpers in Acts and the Epistles. Then, through Paul, God revealed that his mission plan would continue through even more sent ones—gifted leaders who would carry the Great Commission forward by pastoring, planting, connecting, catalyzing, and caring for churches (Ephesians 4:11–13).

Jesus knew that if Great Commission efforts were to continue long after the Twelve and Paul were gone, the Commission must *both* be embraced and supported by all Christians *and* be led forward by gifted leaders—called-out folks beyond the original apostles who would equip, mobilize, and multiply churches "to the end of the age" (Matthew 28:20).

The Four Pillars of Convictional Partnership

Let me tell you something interesting. One of the most comprehensive ministry initiatives among New Testament believers—one that spanned a sizable portion of Paul's ministry—was built around connecting churches.

The Jerusalem collection was the result of numerous small congregations that collaborated across borders for the sake of a single kingdom goal—famine relief for the Jerusalem believers.[3] Paul dedicated ten years of his life to this cause. He connected churches across multiple cities to give to the goal, and when Paul eventually arrived in Jerusalem, envoys from several regions where he planted churches accompanied him. Paul couldn't stop talking about the purpose of this partnership (Romans 15:26; 1 Corinthians 16:1–4; 2 Corinthians 8:1–5; 9:6–15). And it didn't stop with famine relief; we'll explore more of his interchurch strategy for church planting throughout the book.

For Paul, partnership wasn't about growing a ministry or building a brand. No, his goal was to rally diverse churches and harness their resources for greater kingdom impact (2 Corinthians 9:1–2). Why? Paul knew that ministry fruit abounds when churches connect. He grasped a central principle for mission clarity and church vitality: *local churches are stronger together.*

> *For Paul, partnership wasn't about growing a ministry or building a brand. His goal was to rally diverse churches and harness their resources for greater kingdom impact.*

Before moving on, let me say once again, I love the local church. I've been a card-carrying church member for more than forty years, pastored churches for more than three decades, and raised all my kids in the church.

Cut me, and I bleed local church.

But we must not confuse the *priority* of the local church with the *exclusivity* of the local church. To say it another way, the church is *first*, but not *only*.[4] And the difference between these two conclusions can be the difference between flourishing and faltering.

Paul's conviction about the necessity of partnership for the sake of kingdom impact and accomplishing the Great Commission stands on four pillars: (1) Local churches are *knit together* in the gospel; (2) they are *sent together* on mission; (3) they *grow strong together* through a shared theological vision; and (4) they *stay strong together* through ongoing support. Let's unpack these convictions one by one.

Pillar #1: Local churches are knit together in the gospel. When writing to the Philippians about their cooperative efforts, Paul used the term *partnership*. In the introduction of his letter, Paul thanks God for this church: "I thank my God every time I remember you. In all my prayers for all of you, I always pray with joy because of your *partnership in the gospel* from the first day until now" (1:3–5 NIV, emphasis mine).

It's counterintuitive. The Philippians were a strong church, yet they were not an autonomous church. Though this church had established elders and deacons (1:1), they remained vitally connected with a leadership entity *outside* of their local elders. The Philippians remained connected to Paul and his carefully selected helpers.[5] Their maturity did not fortify their *independence*, but rather their *interdependence*.[6]

The joy Paul describes in Philippians 1 is not based on a mutual love for a sports team or style of music; this joy is found in the deep fellowship experienced between Paul and the church through their *partnership*. Paul's joy springs from the unity they experience in the life-transforming news of God's kingdom breaking into this world through the person and work of Jesus Christ. The gospel is not simply information; it is a dynamic, unstoppable force that God has unleashed in creation through the cross.[7]

Moreover, this partnership flows from a deep well of confidence in the reality we are not only forgiven individually by Jesus, but we are now adopted corporately into God's family. Now, as a result, we are called to the family enterprise—putting Christ's message into circulation (Matthew 28:16–20). As Chris

Bruno and Matt Dirks write, "The gospel unites leaders and churches in a way that no philosophy, tradition, task, or mission ever could. People who understand their need and desperate dependence on God's grace are naturally drawn to one another . . . And that kind of gospel fellowship is where every great partnership starts."[8]

Paul tells us it is the gospel that motivated his work. After giving thanks for the Philippians' partnership in the gospel and expressing confidence that the one who began a good work in this church would be faithful to complete it (Philippians 1:3–6), Paul says, "It is right for me to feel this way about you all, because I hold you in my heart, *for you are all partakers with me of grace*" (v. 7, emphasis mine).

Conversion certainly begins as a "God and me" experience, but Paul knows it can't end there. Why? Because all Christians are partakers together of a common grace. Paul's connection with the Philippians flowed from a deep well of confidence that they had not only been forgiven by Jesus individually, but that they were now part of God's one family. As Dane Ortlund says:

> We live our lives in Christ in a way that is vitally, organically joined to all other believers. We who are in Christ are no more detached from other believers than muscle tissue can be detached from ligaments in a healthy body. When you pass another Christian in the grocery store or in the hallway at church, that is a body's hand passing that same body's foot, both of whom are controlled by a single head. They may be different genders, different ethnicities, polar opposite personalities, and seventy years apart in age—but they are far more connected than two siblings from the same family, ethnic background, and DNA, one of whom is in Christ while the other is not.[9]

When we embrace this corporate nature of the gospel promise, we move out beyond *our own church's thing* and think more about what it means to be on mission *together*. In the same way individual Christians who experience renewal seek relationships for service and connection, so also churches that desire gospel renewal pursue affiliation and cooperation. They know that the gospel has knit them together, so they seek to unite their lives and resources to bless other churches and then bear gospel witness to the world. That delivers us to the second pillar.

Pillar #2: Local churches are sent together on mission. Ever rolled over in your mind the claim Acts 1:8 makes on the church? "You will be my witnesses *in Jerusalem and in all Judea and Samaria, and to the end of the earth*" (emphasis added).

The reality is that when any leader or church leadership team soberly considers the global sweep of the Great Commission, they must conclude that no single church, tribe, or denomination is going to ever accomplish it alone. To satisfy the Great Commission, we need church cooperation. Louis Berkhof echoed Reformation thinking when he wrote, "The Reformed system . . . maintains the right and duty of the local church to unite with similar churches on a common confessional basis, and form a wider organization for doctrinal, judicial, and administrative purposes."[10]

In saying this, we are hardly pioneering new ground. In the seventeenth century, Puritan John Cotton advocated for the liberty of communion with other churches for the propagation or multiplication of churches,[11] and in 1744, the Baptist Association in Charleston, South Carolina, declared, "In order the more amply to obtain this blessing of communion, there ought to be a coalescing or uniting of several churches into one body, so far as their local situation and other circumstances will admit."[12]

If Acts and the rest of the New Testament represent a chronicle of how the disciples understood and applied the Great Commission, it was the partnership between local churches and extra-local ministries (Ephesians 4:11–13) that pushed the gospel out. In the New Testament, local churches remained *local*, while ministries like that of Paul and his helpers were *mobile*.[13]

The church authorized and partnered with qualified people who helped extend the mission to new places. In today's terms, it's a pioneer missions organization that travels to places where Christ has not been named. It's also a church planting network that helps plant and build local churches.[14] A network exists, in fact, to balance the tension between God's local design for elder-led congregations and his global design for vitally connected churches. Missiologist Paul Hiebert put it this way: "The future of missions is based in the formation of international networks rather than 'multinational organizations.' Networks build up people, not programs; they stress partnership and servanthood, not hierarchy; they help to build up the local church, not undermine it."[15]

Networks are voluntary associations, not hierarchical obligations—as denominations can sometimes become. They are flexible, dynamic, and nimble.[16] They are largely focused, not on organizational growth, but rather on strengthening and equipping churches for mission.

Here's the pattern I see in Scripture, which I'm advocating for throughout this book: Organizations don't plant churches, nor do churches alone plant churches. Partnerships plant churches! Thus, we arrive at a critical *both/and* in Paul's missiology. For Paul, "partnership" described *both* how Paul connected to the churches *and* how Paul connected churches.

Paul had about thirty-eight helpers he traveled with at different times in his church planting efforts. These men and women acted as an extra-local group that united the efforts of churches to plant churches and strengthen believers. And the Philippians understood they were called into this gospel partnership with Paul—summoned by God to help in the apostle's efforts to multiply churches. We'll unpack this more in the next chapter.

Organizations don't plant churches, nor do churches alone plant churches. Partnerships plant churches!

Pillar #3: Local churches grow stronger together by sharing a theological vision. Every church or network has both doctrine (what they believe) and a practical methodology (how they do ministry). In an ideal world, the latter is based on the former. In fact, most leaders tend to assume their methodology flows from the undiluted pool of their theology. I certainly did. I believed our elder meetings, mission efforts, benevolence ministry, and small groups operated as they did because that's what we understood the Scriptures to say. When another church differed with us methodologically but shared the same confession, we wondered what had gone wrong. Can you relate?

The truth is that there's an often-undiscovered bridge between our theology and our practice. The term *theological vision* was conceived by theologian Richard Lints and then popularized by pastor Timothy Keller to describe the particular vison for what a local church is going to do with their doctrine in a particular time and place.[17] Our theological vision crystalizes when we prayerfully reflect on both *the gospel* and *our context*—the people among whom, the place where, and the time when we are doing the work of ministry.

Keller thinks of theological vision in terms of how

computers are built. If your doctrinal convictions (your creeds, confessions, and statement of faith) are your hardware, and your ministry expressions (church programs, strategies, and methods) are your software, then your theological vision is the "middleware"—the unseen layer of code that helps your operating system run seamlessly.[18] It's like a mental editor to examine your core beliefs about the gospel, culture, and people and then to propose how those beliefs might be wisely applied to your target audience. It's the set of assumptions you make about doctrine and culture that control how you will apply your theology practically.

With Keller and others, I share the conviction that the true baseline for unity within a network is rooted in *clarity and agreement around a shared theological vision.* This is a delicate matter because a theological vision is often assumed rather than stated. Networks often ask planters, churches, and partners to affirm their statement of faith and cultural values. Others raise the bar by evaluating a potential partner's relational and methodological fit. Yet if the theological vision—the set of assumptions that drives ministry—remains undiscussed and unaffirmed, unity hasn't really been achieved.[19]

In their book *Together for the City,* Neil Powell and John James write the following:

> The driving force behind establishing a cause around which to partner is the theological vision. That vision establishes the nature of a church's ministry expressions, and among them a common cause emerges, around which a number of churches with the same vision can begin to coalesce. So theological vision is the glue that holds a movement of diverse churches together. It allows churches to serve a movement rather than simply seek to multiply churches in

their own image. The sum is far greater than the parts, and the results are diverse.[20]

To illustrate this, when the leadership of Great Commission Collective (GCC), the network I serve as president, considered our own approach to theology and practice, we settled on a theological vision with four fixed categories: Gospel + Collective + Multiplication + Longevity. Keller's Redeemer City to City network uses the categories of Gospel + City + Movement.

Pillar #4: Local churches stay strong together through ongoing support. As we follow Paul's travels in the book of Acts, a beautiful pattern emerges. Paul established a church in a location (often an urban and commercial center). He sometimes lingered there, and then he moved on to plant another church in a new city or region.

But Paul was not a serial entrepreneur, launching the project and then hitting the exit. No, he often returned to the new church plants to invest in their spiritual formation, nourish his relationship with them, and bring reports about the gospel's work through them to other connected churches.[21] His mission was broad, and it involved more than church planting and frontier mission initiatives. "One feature of Paul's missionary activity," observes Charles Wanamaker, "was to link his various missionary churches together on a regional basis so that they would provide mutual support."[22]

Our extra-local work today must also be applied in a way that fosters local church health, soul-enriching relationships, the presence of fruitful ministries, and the support necessary to sustain mission effectiveness over the long haul. As you may have noticed in the summary of our theological vision above, this reality has shaped our identity at GCC. We exist to *plant churches and strengthen leaders*. In other words, our purpose is not simply missional; it's also developmental and relational.

This broader definition of mission is what we find in Paul's use of the word *koinonia* for "partnership" in Philippians 1:5. Paul's usage is rich with warm relational tones. Just listen to Paul's heart for the Philippians:

> I thank my God in all my remembrance of you . . . making my prayer with joy . . . It is right for me to feel this way about you all, because I hold you in my heart . . . For God is my witness, how I yearn for you all with the affection of Christ Jesus. (Philippians 1:3–4, 7–8)

Paul doesn't merely address the Philippian leadership as a group of ministry professionals he's seeking to mobilize for gospel expansion. He speaks to leaders he knows and loves. A *koinonia*—a partnering fellowship—is bound up in intentional brotherhood.[23] Paul's ongoing connection with the Philippian church was one of nourishment and strengthening. As Peter O'Brien explains, "Proclaiming the gospel meant for Paul not simply an initial preaching or with it the reaping of converts; it included also a whole range of nurture and strengthening activities which led to the firm establishment of congregations."[24]

Paul doesn't merely address the Philippian leadership as a group of ministry professionals he's seeking to mobilize for gospel expansion. He speaks to leaders he knows and loves.

Jake desperately needs this. He planted a church two years ago, and it has been an exhilarating ride. His new church is growing faster than expected. But while the church is thriving, Jake has been troubled. He spent so much time starting the church that he never considered what it meant to shepherd the people who came. He never considered how much quick growth could complicate church life. If you spotted Jake around town, you would detect the early warning signs of burnout.

If we want to move toward the Pauline paradigm, we must call participant churches to more than mission. We need both the front-end activities of sending and planting, as well as the follow-up activities that nourish leaders like Jake. Our goals should go beyond a strong or well-financed start to building with longevity in view.

That's why Paul deploys Timothy and Epaphroditus in Philippi (Philippians 2:19–30). His goal for the Philippians wasn't transactional. It wasn't simply for them to spin off churches. No, Paul was concerned for their welfare (v. 20). He wanted this church to be joyfully cheered up by the support they'd receive from ministers who were also their friends (vv. 19, 28).

It's becoming more common today for groups to define success almost exclusively through the mission of church planting. The impulse to plant churches is noble and certainly attracts entrepreneurial leaders, at least at first. But it's the camaraderie and sharpening through networks that keep church leaders committed to networks over the long haul. Wise network leaders recognize that healthy and connected pastors are ultimately the best assets in mobilizing churches for mission.

Paul saw this. He remembered and strengthened the churches through follow-up; it was part of a strategic ministry pattern that's clear throughout the New Testament.[25] And this ministry fellowship was reciprocal.

The churches were asked to pray for Paul's ministry.[26] They received detailed updates about his extra-local mission.[27] They welcomed extra-local leaders with hospitality.[28] And they developed and sent out missional leaders themselves.[29]

Beware the Vice: Consumerism

Partnership swarms with benefits. For church planting networks, it's the benefits that are often most attractive to the church that considers affiliation. But in the Western world, church leaders can't wake up in the morning without chugging the coffee of consumerism. Consumerism transforms partnership into an arrangement where the supplier (the network) meets an on-demand market need (shared theology, care and counseling, missional strategy) for the customer (the church). The customer then measures key performance indicators (KPI, or fruit) to evaluate the return on investment (ROI, usually numerical or financial growth).

For networks, this means the questions leaders ask often start with *consumer interests*: Can this network provide the help, support, and opportunities we're looking for? What kind of value will a partnership deliver to us?

I get it. You wouldn't choose a stock fund if you knew it was going to dive and jeopardize every penny you invested. And you probably shouldn't choose a church planting network if it's not going to help the ministry and mission of your church. Basic biblical principles of stewardship legitimize these questions and remind leaders that fruit should result from any partnership.

But the decision to partner must start with realities that are larger than the unmet needs of the individual leader or the church they represent. Partnerships must be measured by kingdom metrics. The natural man builds earthly organizations where value is measured only by what it acquires. But God's calculator for value works by what flows to and from the soul in both giving and receiving. To God, partnership is bountiful because it's biblical and the blessing flows both ways.

Committing to the humility and service required for inter-dependent church partnerships certainly nourishes the souls of both pastors and people. But as it is with our daily meals, sometimes we live aware of the nourishment, and yet often we do not. Regardless, our fundamental drive must be the pattern in the Bible, not the calculation of our benefits.

I'm not trying to drive down expectations for networks. They exist because of the overwhelming benefits. But some pastors approach church planting networks in transactional ways they would never want replicated by members of their church. I mean, if we're being honest, most pastors would instinctively stiffen if a church member hammered them about the ROI (return on investment) for their giving. We'd try to guide the congregant away from the clear consumerism underlying such transactional thinking. But when pastors approach giving to a partnership, it's not uncommon to treat the conversation like we're negotiating for a used car.

Vice Audit 1: Consumerism

Rank the degree to which you agree with the following statements on a scale of 1–5 (5 = strongly agree, 4 = agree, 3 = neutral, 2 = disagree, 1 = strongly disagree). Write your ranking in the blank to the left of each statement.

_____ 1. Our attitude toward network partnership is driven more by the calculation of benefits (or consumer interests) our church might receive as our return on our investment.

_____ 2. The conscience of our leadership team would be clear if our church was completely independent, with no outside network or denominational affiliation.

_____ 3. The opportunity we have to give to gospel missions rarely factors into our evaluation of our network or denominational partnership.

_____ 4. When we joined our network, our hopes that the partnership would help us grow numerically and financially were the primary drivers behind our decision.

_____ 5. We find ourselves regularly disappointed with the fact we're giving more than we feel we receive from our network.

_____ **Total**

If your church and leadership scored between 0–8, you likely have strongly held Great Commission convictions. If you scored between 9–18, take some time to sit with your leadership team and talk through the four pillars in this chapter. If you scored between 19–25, your church is in danger of succumbing to the vice of consumerism. Take some time to confess this to the Lord and pray that God will help you develop a local church culture that values his mission beyond your church.

Partnerships have enormous value first because they are biblical and then because interdependent churches can achieve together what no one church can accomplish alone. Often the value quantifies easily. Other times, network leaders must talk like George Bailey at the Bedford Falls Building and Loan. In the movie *It's a Wonderful Life*, the people rush to the bank to withdraw their money, but George jumps up to tell them to hang on, to realize that the real resources aren't locked away in a vault; they're in what we do together. "The money's not here, Sam. It's in Joe's church and Bill's and a hundred others. *You're* lending them the money to build, and they're going to pay it back to you as best they can."[30]

> "*The money's not here, Sam. It's in Joe's church and Bill's and a hundred others.*"

George persuaded his customers that the Building and Loan was valuable because they were investing together to move one another forward. That takes time.

Let's face it. Problems emerge when the ROI impulse drives the first or central set of questions about partnership. Where consumerism is not buffered by other values and convictions, it reframes partnerships into transactional arrangements. Family relationships become mercenary, a work for hire. The question of "What do we get?" replaces more noble instincts like "What can we build together?"

Conviction Engenders Commitment

Conviction is different from consumerism. When pastors and church leaders are convinced *churches are stronger together*, they'll throw themselves wholeheartedly into mutual commitments.

Here's what I believe. God is most glorified, not when his people fixate on their advantages, but when partners spend themselves in fulfillment of their promises. Biblical love, after all, does not keep accounts or measure who is most invested at each stage of a relationship. Rather, it keeps sacrifice at the center. This is because partnerships exist to reflect the covenant-keeping nature of our promise-keeping God. I love the way George Peters describes it:

> Partnership in missions is a sacred and comprehensive concept of equals bound together in mutual confidence, unified purpose and unified effort, accepting equal responsibilities, authority, praise and blame; sharing burdens, joys, sorrows, victories and defeats. It means joint planning, joint legislation, joint programming, and involves the sending and receiving of churches on an equal basis. Only the closest bond in Christ, savored by a rich measure of humility, love, confidence and self-giving, will actualize partnership.[31]

Though it is possible for a church to survive in isolation, survival is too small of a goal. Perhaps churches could move faster and more efficiently by themselves. But if you remain determined to follow the New Testament pattern, you'll find your heart committing to a partnership grounded in this conviction: *local churches are stronger together.*

Biblical love does not keep accounts, or measure who is most invested at each stage of a relationship. Rather, it keeps sacrifice at the center.

VIRTUE

GIFTED
LEADERSHIP

Against Isolationism

Have you ever heard of C. C. McCabe? Folks called him "Two-a-Day McCabe"—an odd moniker for an old Methodist. But in the world of church planting, he was a beast. With McCabe as the denomination's church extension secretary (think church planting director today) in the late 1800s, the Methodists were already averaging one church per day.

Then, while on a train to the Pacific Northwest, C. C. McCabe picked up a newspaper. In it he read the account of a speech by Robert Ingersoll, known as "the Great Agnostic," delivered the prior day in Chicago. Ingersoll had boldly exclaimed, "The churches are dying out all over the land; they are struck with death."

If Ingersoll was hoping to plant doubts within the Methodist movement, his speech had the opposite effect. Instead, Ingersoll had unknowingly punched McCabe's passion button. At the very next station, the church planting leader stepped off the train and sent this telegram:

Dear Robert,

All hail the power of Jesus' name! We are building more than one Methodist church every day in the year and [now] propose to make it two a day!

C. C. McCabe[1]

A report of the telegram circulated, and it electrified McCabe's denominational base. Eventually, the message was enshrined in a hymn written by Alfred J. Hough:

> The infidels, a motley band,
> In council met, and said:
> "The Churches die all through the land,
> The last will soon be dead."
> When suddenly a message came,
> It filled them with dismay:
> "All hail the power of Jesus' name!
> We're building *two* a day."[2]

McCabe then seized on the lyrics and leveraged it to inspire more faith for church planting.

"This song immediately spread like fire over the land," said one biographer, "and [McCabe] sang it from ocean to ocean, and by its note of faith and victory the song . . . gave a new and wonderful impetus to all the benevolent enterprises of the Church."[3]

Church history is peppered with men like C. C. McCabe—those who see the boasts of agnostics as opportunities for mission. These persons[4] seize on setbacks and make them advances. They break open new gospel ground, form movements, and inspire entire denominations to sing about the glories of gospel progress.

There's a reason for this. When God wants to spread the glory of Christ's substitutionary sacrifice, he taps a particular kind of leader. The history of Christian movements is not largely a story of the masses organizing effectively to see the gospel advanced; it's the story of bold leadership.

The history of Christian movements is not largely a story of the masses organizing effectively to see the gospel advanced; it's the story of bold leadership.

Behold the Virtue:
Gifted Extra-Local Leadership

Paul tells us that God has gifted the church with people who are set apart in various leadership roles—to lead local churches, to lead groups of churches toward broader gospel expansion, and to lead churches in consolidated ministry efforts. We read about these leaders in Ephesians 4:11–13 (emphasis mine):

> And he gave *the apostles, the prophets, the evangelists, the shepherds and teachers*, to equip the saints for the work of ministry, for building up the body of Christ, until we all attain to the unity of the faith and of the knowledge of the Son of God, to mature manhood, to the measure of the stature of the fullness of Christ.

The very first gift in this list is that of the apostle. If we are going to understand the people who form and drive church planting networks,[5] we must be willing to discuss this gift. There are several observations we can make about Ephesians 4 that will help us understand the apostolic gift.

First, the passage is time-stamped. All the gifts listed here— from pastor to apostle—are necessary "until we all attain to the unity of the faith and of the knowledge of the Son of God." That is to say, these gifts remain active and strategic until Christ returns.[6]

Second, the passage is forward-looking. The Twelve will always hold a unique place in the purposes of God (Revelation 21:14). As will Paul too, since he received the gospel and his commission directly from the risen Christ. If the Twelve were a professional basketball team, Paul would be the thirteenth guy on the bench, and after him, the roster would be closed. His unique role in redemptive history should be seen as distinct, exceptional, and unrepeatable (Galatians 1:12; Ephesians 3:3).[7] This is not to say there are zero points of continuity between Paul and present-day ministry. I'll talk about the continuity below. But for now, it's important to establish that Paul and the Twelve were irreplaceable, one-of-a-kind, capital-A Apostles.

But the Ephesians 4:11 passage is not looking back to the Twelve and Paul. They are not the ones in view here. This passage is looking forward. It shifts our gaze beyond this group to a less foundational but not insignificant group of "apostles."[8] The New Testament expands the semantic range of the word *apostle*[9] to include others who did not possess the authority of Paul or the Twelve but whose primary function was the planting and establishing of churches.[10] I understand this to mean that the Great Commission work of the first, authoritative apostles continues beyond their lifetimes through the work of other Ephesians 4 leaders, particularly those with a continuing function as "sent ones."

In 1973, missiologist Ralph Winter delivered a monumental message at a mission conference in Korea. He described two redemptive structures reflected in Scripture and church history. He labeled them the *modality* (the local church) and the *sodality* (mission societies and other Ephesians 4 ministries).

Both structures, Winter argued, were legitimate, and each one "corresponded faithfully to the function of patterns Paul employed."[11] Winter even argued that the genetics of the Protestant tradition—featuring a more exclusive modality-mindedness—implanted a DNA that decidedly weakened its mission effectiveness. By advocating for sodalities, Winter called the church to recognize that Christ is still at work distributing Ephesian 4 gifts.

I agree with Winter that there is biblical warrant for extra-local ministry teams ("the apostles, the prophets, the evangelists") that exist alongside local church leaders ("the shepherds and teachers") to serve those churches in their mission.

Third, the passage makes leadership gifts a fruit of the gospel. Paul makes clear earlier in Ephesians 4 exactly where gifted leaders find their origin and purpose. Jesus descended to earth in the incarnation, lived in full compliance to the law, died a substitutionary death, and was raised on the third day in victory. Now he has ascended to the right hand of the Father. Just as a birthday party means gift giving, Jesus' resurrection and ascension mean the same. The living and enthroned Christ now gives gifted leaders to his church (Ephesians 4:7–9). These gifts are a fruit of the gospel. Paul's theology here is a riff on what Jesus said to his disciples in John 20:21: "As the Father has sent me, even so I am sending you."

Finally, while Paul's place was unique, his ministry nevertheless provides the compass for understanding the apostolic gift named in Ephesians 4. Vern Poythress once offered a helpful way to distinguish between New Testament and modern gifts. "I maintain," says Poythress, "that modern gifts are analogous to but not identical with the divinely authoritative gifts exercised by the apostles."[12]

As I briefly discussed in the first chapter, it's in the ministry of Paul that we are given the clearest model for our ongoing mission. Paul's role was distinct, but his ministry still rings with relevance for church planting today. As we seek to plant churches and build interdependent networks of churches, we see two specific points of continuity between Paul's Great Commission pattern and our church planting efforts today— the *message* and the *model.*

- **The message.** Paul's partnership with the Philippians was a "*partnership in the gospel* from the first day until now" (1:5, emphasis mine). The glorious message of Christ's perfect life, sacrificial death, exultant resurrection, and awe-inspiring ascension forms a nexus where the mission of every Christian and that of the gifted Ephesians 4 leaders connect to Paul. "We believe that it is the gospel of our Lord Jesus Christ within God's purposes," says P. T. O'Brien, "that serve as *the bridge between Paul's own missionary activity and that of others.* The apostolic kerygma appears to be the *critical link* between the two."[13]

  Just consider what this means. The message proclaimed by Paul is the very same message we carry—the same power, transformational impact, and liberating effects in the lives of hearers. Charles Spurgeon's grandfather once said of his grandson, the Prince of Preachers, "He may preach the gospel better than I can, but he cannot preach a better gospel."[14] Let this encourage your soul. We carry the same good news that the apostles did. When we place the gospel at the center of our churches and networks, it will deliver the same transformational power.

- **The model.** "The narrative of Paul's missionary work," writes Eckhard Schnabel, "provides a paradigm, a model for the mission of the church."[15] As we follow Paul's ministry in the New Testament, we see a beautiful pattern emerge. Paul and his team applied the Great Commission by *multiplying churches through partnership.* Their extra-local ministry led to interconnectedness among the churches, to the strengthening and encouragement of the churches toward maturity, and to serving churches in various other ways that transcended a single congregation.[16] Perhaps these churches could have survived on their own, but the New Testament confirms they were stronger together. They gave generously to the poor together, contended for orthodox theology together, and helped plant more churches throughout the Mediterranean together.

Every generation of leaders must strive to enjoy the kind of fruitful interdependence that reproduces this biblical pattern. Paul's ministry provides a model for the mission-minded interdependence reflected in some denominations and networks today. A modern-day apostle's function is similar to Paul's, but it's missiological, not governmental. Today's apostolic-type leaders are copies, not the originals. As such, they dwell in the beautiful tension between local church autonomy and God-given extra-local influence. Where apostolic leaders—sent ones—and their gifts are welcome, they help local church leaders see the world outside and move toward it with missional determination.

Why It Matters

I fully recognize that "apostle talk" creates a visceral reaction among some, and for good reason. Why not just run an advertisement to fast-track guys straight into egotism, celebrity, and unaccountable influence! For this reason (and others), some Christian theologians maintain the complete cessation of the apostolic role. Gregg Allison, for instance, writes, "I maintain that the office of apostleship was unique and temporary, divinely designed to be formative for the early church and then to cease with the death of the last apostle"[17] Leaders like Allison are seeking to protect the integrity of the canon and minimize the potential abuses of authority that are unleashed when we leave the door cracked to apostolic language. I hear their concerns, and I'm sympathetic to their position.

In view of these realities, it bears repeating that there are fixed, unrepeatable features of the capital-A Apostolic office that are reserved for the Twelve and Paul. They had a unique role in writing the New Testament Scriptures and unique authority that they exercised over "all the churches" (1 Corinthians 7:17–24; 14:29–35; 1 Thessalonians 3:14–15). We shouldn't make the mistake of giving apostolic authority to any individual today—no matter how gifted they appear to be or how much mission momentum they seem to generate!

> *We shouldn't make the mistake of giving apostolic authority to any individual today—no matter how gifted they appear to be or how much mission momentum they seem to generate!*

Nevertheless, I believe it's important for the church to affirm a continuing apostolic function in sent leaders with extra-local influence. Setting aside gifted extra-local leaders remains the most effective way for local churches to carry out their broader mission. Whenever a local church partners with a mission organization, network, or denominational entity, they are partnering with leaders who have been gifted by the Spirit and recognized by the church to serve as extra-local catalysts. My argument is that there is biblical warrant for the existence of these extra-local ministry teams that walk alongside local churches to serve them and help them participate in God's larger mission.

The existence of an apostolic role given to those who are set apart for the broader mission helps explain why the New Testament does not encourage elders to train every believer to leave home and go to the nations. In New Testament missions, it's those gifted for apostolic function who go. As George Miley observes, "Most Christians will not leave home and go someplace else to minister."[18] The local church remains local.

I have affinity with Timothy Keller, who doesn't see Ephesians 4 as describing five abiding, distinct roles given to the church but nevertheless appeals to the extra-local role of "bishop" that John Calvin described in his *Institutes of the Christian Religion*. As Keller says, "It was almost as if Calvin, while believing that the apostolic office had ceased, nevertheless saw that some had unusual gifts of leadership that should be recognized."[19]

These gifts *should* be recognized. In fact, I believe that identifying and releasing extra-local ministry gifts is one of the most strategic things the church can do to advance mission today.[20] Here is a summary of what I'm arguing for, with a few practical handles for churches and leaders:

- We should advocate for an apostolic function in a way that protects the unique and unrepeatable role of the Twelve and Paul.[21]
- We should see the apostolic function as a gift, not an office.[22]
- We should use the apostolic pattern, not the title.
- We can expand our understanding of the Great Commission by saying, "The Eleven received it and the church finishes it *by partnering with gifted persons for mission and strengthening.*"

Behold the Vice: Isolationism

The opposite can also happen. When a church neglects gifted leadership or feeds on a local community emphasis with no extra-local connections, that church can grow inward, insular, and self-absorbed. It's the vice of *isolationism*, and its causes can be judged with a variety of verdicts—sometimes the motives are innocent, and at other times there is legitimate guilt.

Isolationism verdict # 1: Innocent, but in need of gifted help. The pastors at Faith Church were wired for shepherding. Missional thinking just wasn't in their tool kit. As a result, their church cultivated some remarkable strengths in care, teaching, and richly connected relationships. The elders, however, detected a hazardous trend. Faith Church was becoming an *ingrown* church—focusing so deliberately on their fellowship and local needs that they lived largely unconscious of God's larger mission. Their *koinonia* had become *koinonitis*; community inflammation had blocked the blood flow of mission.[23]

Sometimes churches grow inward because that's simply how the church's leaders are wired. The truth is that shepherds alone don't tend to multiply churches. I'm not throwing shade on the church eldership here. Healthy elders are essential to a healthy church, but elders have specific gifts, burdens, and limitations. Their leadership tends to flow toward care, teaching, protection, and stability . . . and for that, we thank God!

Shepherds alone don't tend to multiply churches.

But there are two weaknesses that elders often share. In fact, when you see the eldership profile that forms from the prerequisites in 1 Timothy 3 and Titus 1, you get it. Elders tend to be risk averse and lack mission motivation. It makes sense. Because elders are called by God to shepherd and disciple people in a particular place, their passions don't tend to flow toward accepting the risks involved with starting new works and advancing missions. If your elders have a vision to plant churches, you need to thank God even as you recognize it as the exception, not the rule.

Network leaders, have you had this experience? You sit across the table from lead pastors or elders who boast that their team and members love their local church too much to leave it. They perceive the centripetal energy that spins the church inward as a commendation of their efforts. More and more resources flow toward maintaining what has been built, which syncs well with the burdens of most elders and pastors. Those burdens tend to be *upward* (in worship) and *inward* (in community and discipleship), not *outward* (in mission).[24] But a local church cannot be truly healthy when a heart for mission is conspicuously absent and the fruit of this omission is celebrated as a strength.

When the pastors of Faith Church saw that they needed help, they joined a church planting network. Through honest conversations with gifted leaders in the network, the illness was quickly diagnosed. The church's elders were armed with treatments, and two potential church planters were soon identified. Three years later, Faith Church stands on the threshold of sending out their second church planter.

If your elders—because of their shepherd/teacher giftings and focus—have been unable to advocate for the outward impulse, they should seek help from church planting ministries. They must begin to identify those from outside the body—and perhaps even those within the body—who have Ephesians 4 gifts. They must find those whom God is sending.[25]

Isolationism verdict #2: Innocent, but in need of connection. It's the battle cry of many networks and denominations today: *churches plant churches.* For those who use the phrase to describe how interdependent churches can partner to multiply,

I say, "Preach it!" But for those who use it to mean local churches multiplying through catalytic elders, I say, "Sure, that probably happens *occasionally*." But statistically it's rare. The statement would be closer to reality if it read, *Large churches with catalytic leaders plant churches. Sometimes.*

One renowned missiologist observed, "The history of the church in missions is in the main the history of great personalities and of missionary societies. Only in exceptional cases has it been the church in missions."[26] For most churches to plant churches, they need vital partnerships with apostolically gifted ministries that will help inspire their will and inform their way.

The networks that have adopted the "churches plant churches" approach are seeking a good thing. They want to protect the centrality of the local church and the Great Commission's place in the local church. I commend the desire. But we can't neglect the testimony of history or overexaggerate how most churches roll. Partnerships exist so that local churches can get vitally involved in church planting. But we must keep our eye on a vital point introduced in chapter 1: *Churches don't really plant churches; partnerships do.*

We must see that the churches in the New Testament did not partner together randomly. Rather, the early churches actually connected through the agency of extra-local workers like Paul and his helpers (2 Corinthians 9:1–2; 1 Thessalonians 1:8).[27] The extra-local role became a key point of continuity between the churches. The churches were not restricted to connecting through Paul. God just used Paul's role and gifts to better facilitate it.

Throughout church history, gifted leaders have emerged within churches regionally, nationally, and internationally to mobilize partnerships for mission. Like Paul, extra-local leaders have facilitated church relationships as part of their service. They have been essential and effective tools for connecting churches in both local and global mission partnerships and for training ministers in specialized ways.[28]

Isolationism verdict #3: Guilty, as a result of pride. My cousin tried to tell me, "Put on the emergency brake!" But, of course, I knew best. Sure, it was her dad's car and she had been driving it for years. But I dismissed her with a wave. Five minutes later, I received word that my uncle's GTO was rolling backward down a hill. It had been stopped by three providentially placed teens just seconds before it would have made impact with another vehicle.

Thankfully, Jesus' unstoppable love displayed through his unspeakable death saved me from blind self-obsession. But to this day, one Bible passage makes me relive that story: "In those days there was no king in Israel. Everyone did what was right in his own eyes" (Judges 17:6). Before knowing Jesus, I thought folks were wise if they agreed with me and foolish if they didn't. Like the Israelites in the days of the judges, I wouldn't receive counsel from anyone—elders, friends, or *cousins*—if they said something that clouded the sparkle of my own pride.

Sometimes the biggest thing standing between our church and the mission field is our unwillingness to acknowledge our need for help—though it's something I've had to do more times than I can count. And each time, there's a skirmish in my soul as I wage war with the pride that tells me to never telegraph my weakness or need. The Devil—our common foe—loves to persuade leaders that they can do everything on their own and in their own way.

Proud folks never play well in the network sandbox. After all, interdependence means being challenged by new leaders, new ideas, new methods, and people who are less than impressed with our methods, models, and church achievements. It's far more appealing to the flesh to just run our playbook and avoid questions that may challenge our omniscience. But when churches connect with each other and new influences are welcomed into the lives of staff, elders, and lead pastors, a team gains catalytic influence and helpful accountability—colleagues who aren't impressed by your church fruit and aren't burdened by the trappings of having to report to you (Galatians 2:11–14).

Elders exercise real authority and true responsibility. When addressing a proud leader, a network is no replacement for a wise plurality of church leaders. But network assistance can make a real difference. The wise lead pastor recognizes he has two ears to hear two voices—those of his plurality and his network. The network voice is highly significant for mission and remarkably helpful when a church leadership team is navigating ministry complexities.

Sometimes a team of elders needs a gifted third-party leader to help them understand their role. Sometimes that person will inform their clarity and incite their courage. At times, it's an outside voice that encourages the leadership team to hold a senior leader accountable—which leads us to the final isolationism verdict.

Isolationism verdict #4: Guilty, due to a lack of accountability. Gifted leaders who are untethered from truth-speaking relationships are a significant cause of isolationism. And when their unaccountable practices become public fodder, Christians become disillusioned, churches falter, and entire movements fail.

I recently listened to a podcast titled *The Rise and Fall of Mars Hill*, a twelve-episode series produced by *Christianity Today*.[29] The program follows the ministry of Seattle pastor Mark Driscoll. Words fail in trying to describe the haunting shadow cast by this story. While the series was not without its flaws, it formed a sobering, instructive, and cautionary tale of what happens when the meteoric rise of an Ephesians 4 gift eclipses the church, the elders, and any meaningful accountability.

At the conclusion of each episode, two competing thoughts rolled through my head: First, *Mark Driscoll was a genius.* Second, *Mark Driscoll should have listened to more non-geniuses.* And even when the best and brightest did weigh in, there was no one under which "his genius [was] rebuked."[30]

Driscoll is just another name in the catalog of remarkably gifted people who have started ministries, launched networks, and published books while surrounding themselves with little to no accountability. Sometimes they ditch the local elders and assemble a group of friends or peers outside of the church; sometimes they just ditch the elders. But the pattern of catalytic leaders standing alone—in charge but unchallenged, celebrated but unaccountable—is not simply a disease; it's a pandemic. As Thabiti Anyabwile makes clear, "Accountability is essential—and not just passive, reactionary accountability but searching, probing, initiative-taking accountability."[31] That's why I will talk about it more in chapter 6.

Vice Audit 2: Isolationism

Rank the degree to which you agree with the following statements on a scale of 1–5 (5 = strongly agree, 4 = agree, 3 = neutral, 2 = disagree, 1 = strongly disagree). Write your ranking in the blank to the left of each statement.

_____ 1. There are more leaders on our team who are gifted for care, teaching, protection, and stability than there are leaders who are gifted for catalyzing mission efforts.

45

_____ 2. I tend to believe that our church can catalyze mission efforts apart from a partnership with gifted leaders outside of our local church.

_____ 3. Our team finds it more appealing to just run our own ministry playbook without being challenged by new leaders, new ideas, new methods, or people who are less impressed with our methods, models, or church achievements.

_____ 4. The leaders on our team are untethered from small groups where people know them. They are not connected to truth-speaking relationships where their attitudes and behaviors can be regularly challenged.

_____ 5. It's rare for our church to recognize leaders from within our congregation who could plant a church or are gifted and called to bless the larger church.

_____ **Total**

If your church and leadership scored between 0–8, you likely have a healthy understanding of gifted extra-local leadership. If you scored between 9–18, take some time to sit with your leadership team and talk through the isolationism verdicts in this chapter. If you scored between 19–25, your church is in danger of succumbing to the vice of isolationism. Take some time to confess this to the Lord and begin praying that God will help you to develop a church culture that values accountability and the gifts of extra-local leaders.

In the risky, high-stakes world of missions—in the rooms where gifted people gather—accountability seems inconvenient.

Gifted people seem to think it dampens innovation, chills apostolic initiatives, and saps the superpower from outside-the-box thinkers. Accountability checks our independence. And Lord knows how we missional folk love our independence!

Honestly, I think that apostolically gifted, movement-starting, missional persons sometimes twist the definition of accountability. In our minds, we've turned accountability into an overreaching sin fixation that cramps innovation. If this is our definition, accountability becomes a problem, not a solution.[32] As a result, gifted leaders keep rising and then crashing.

It's better to see accountability as a regular practice that should bear the fruit of protection and humility. Yes, accountability is tricky. It's complex. People out in the field don't always have solid local connections within which honest conversations can happen. Parachurch ministries don't always have clear lines for ministry accountability. If network leaders are not also local church elders, they must work much harder to achieve the consistent connections readily available to those leaders.

We've turned accountability into an overreaching sin fixation that cramps innovation. If this is our definition, accountability becomes a problem, not a solution.

But can we agree that accountability is too important to ignore? When conversations about Ephesians 4 ministry begin, one of the biggest fears among thinking Christians is of the damage that has been caused by unaccountable leaders. Advocates of the apostolic function deserve much of this criticism. Here's why. Ephesians 4 people don't tend to practice the interdependence that their gifts were intended to catalyze. But how can one seek to connect the churches if they are not also willing to be accountable to them?

Let me propose a better way. *The more gifted the leader, the more essential the accountability.* Or as Jesus said, "Everyone to whom much was given, of him much will be required" (Luke 12:48). Why? When you have a lot to be proud of, it's more challenging to be humble. Moreover, the margin for error is narrower for a person on whom a lot is riding. Practically speaking, when someone is leading a ministry organization, other people's jobs, income, and career trajectory may be connected to that person's ongoing godliness.

Ask yourself these practical questions: If you are a network leader or denominational executive, are you also a member of a local church? If so, are you involved in a small group where people know you? Does your board take an active role in your care and evaluation? When was the last time someone challenged an attitude or behavior you displayed? When was the last time you confessed sin to another person? Who can your spouse call if they think you've lost the plot?

It makes no sense to sideline the local church in the name of reproducing it elsewhere. Maybe you need to join a small group. Maybe you need to recruit an elder, or a group of two or three people who can invest in your ministry by meeting with you twice a month for accountability. Maybe you need to empower your board with more formal authority to hold you accountable. Humble yourself and strive to embody the principle of accountability. It will protect the people your ministry serves and employs, and it will bring greater credibility to your call for partnership.

A Mission Made Stronger through Gifted Leadership

Partnership through shared leaders is a beautiful thing. Do you remember the hymn written about C. C. McCabe's telegram? Check out the last verse:

When infidels in council meet
Next year, with boastings vain,
To chronicle the Lord's defeat.
And count his Churches slain,
O may we then with joy proclaim,
If we his call obey:
"All hail the power of Jesus' name;
We're building *three* a day."[33]

Don't you love it! The Methodists used the agnostic Robert Ingersoll's words to raise the mission stakes to *three a day*. God used the very gifted C. C. McCabe to inspire them.

It's been that way throughout church history. First-century churches put their convictions about mission into practice when they connected, recognized Ephesians 4 leadership, inspired each other toward growth, and sent out workers to take the gospel to distant lands. They didn't collapse inward with an insular impulse. Instead, they believed it was not good for churches to be alone, and then they chose to partner together through the beautiful virtue of gifted leadership.

PART

2

FINDING YOUR PARTNERSHIP

MAPPING YOUR NETWORK

U p to this point, I've written about how interdependence is the core conviction of church planting networks (chapter 1) and how sharing gifted leadership is necessary for these missional partnerships to thrive (chapter 2). In chapters 3–5, we'll explore collaboration—the way healthy leaders put their convictions about interdependence into practice—and the missional culture that results. Then in the book's final two chapters, we'll discover together the kind of character that is needed to sustain healthy partnership.

But before we move too quickly past the first two chapters, it's important to pause and consider two tensions that network leaders must inhabit. With the help of some smart friends, I've mapped these tensions on what I hope you will experience as an unbiased, evenhanded tool called the Network Matrix.[1]

The Alignment Continuum

The first tension relates to our convictions about interdependence. It's what I'm calling the *alignment continuum*, and it illustrates the way a network balances the emphasis their partnership puts on theology with the emphasis it places on mission.

The Alignment Continuum

Theology ⟵—————————————————⟶ **Mission**

Now it's important to acknowledge that everyone wants to be both theological and missional. Every church planting network has a theology that informs their practice, and every church planting network, by definition, wants to expand. We all want to see the gospel go forth and Jesus magnified through our efforts.

Some church planting networks lead with and organize around theology, while others place the accent on mission. A network that lands on the theological side of the continuum is one that is *leading with what they believe* whereas a partnership that lands on the missional side is *leading with how they impact*. Both groups may be planting churches. But churches on the theology side are multiplying churches with a tighter doctrinal alignment—a more clearly articulated theological vision. Churches on the mission side are generally multiplying churches faster.

The key question here is this: "Which emphasis draws churches or planters to us?" If leaders in a predominantly Calvinistic and Baptist network are perfectly happy to plant churches that, contrary to their theological heritage, practice infant baptism and relish the Wesleyan doctrine of prevenient grace, then that network is leaning toward the mission end of the alignment continuum. But a different network only willing to plant churches with shared theological underpinnings—or even the same core doctrinal statement—will fall more on the theology end of the spectrum.

Some of you already have a network. Perhaps you are reading this book to evaluate that relationship in the hope of strengthening it. Others are looking for a new network partnership. As you answer the questions below, answer them with the network or partnership you are considering in mind.

To plot where your network lands on this continuum, score yourself on the following quiz. Write your score for each question on the line to the left:[2]

_____ Does our network have an agreed-on doctrinal statement, theological vision, or list of core beliefs? Yes (score −1) or No (score +1).

_____ Do new churches or leaders come into the partnership primarily because of their affinity with our theological vision and doctrinal distinctives (score −1)? Or do they enter our network primarily because of their affinity with the way we contextualize and do mission work (score +1)? Score 0 if you are unclear.

_____ Would our network be okay with planting broadly evangelical churches that don't fully agree with some of our core doctrinal statements? Yes (score +1) or No (score −1).

_____ Does the network require that new churches adopt a core doctrinal statement or book of church order that is more particular than the broadly evangelical Lausanne Covenant? Yes (score −1) or No (score +1).

_____ Are churches removed or asked to remove themselves from our partnership when their doctrinal commitments change? Yes (score −1) or No (score +1).

_____ **Total**

Add up your score. If your network scored between -5 and 0, it plots on the theological side of the alignment continuum. If it scored between 0 and 5, your network plots on the missional side. The further your number is from zero, the closer your network is to one of the continuum's edges.

The Structure Continuum

The second tension relates to our convictions about gifted leadership. It's what I call the *structure continuum*. The continuum illustrates the differing levels of involvement and kinds of authority that extra-local leaders (e.g., influential pastors, network staff, denominational leadership) have when new churches are planted. The key question for this continuum is this: "How is power shared?"

The Structure Continuum

Centralized ⟵―――――――――――――――⟶ **Decentralized**

You will find gifted leaders in both centralized and decentralized networks, but two similarly gifted leaders would likely be deployed differently by two networks with differing organizational structures. In fact, these two leaders may in reality be getting their paychecks from different places. In a more centralized network, the gifted leader is more likely to work as an employee of the network. This leader will have more *organizational authority* over the network's work. The goal in consolidating organizational authority and entrusting it to a gifted leader may be the need for expedience, the relative maturity of the group, past polity mistakes, or simply a Spirit-led decision by the network's trustees that organizing in this way will result in greater gains for the kingdom.

In a decentralized network, power and decision making are spread out. The gifted people who drive ministry are often at the local church level, and the authority that is most valued is not a commissioned organizational authority but rather *the authority of influence* that comes because of the relationships key leaders have cultivated. The conviction behind decentralization is that distributing power multiplies ministry.

To plot where your current network or any network partnerships you are considering lands on this continuum, score yourself on the following quiz. Write your score for each question on the line to the left:

_____ Is new growth or expansion initiated by network employees and extra-local leaders (score +1) or by leaders in the churches (score –1)?

_____ Are extra-local leaders required for the assessment and approval of new church planters? Yes (score +1) or No (score –1).

_____ Are new church planters primarily trained by their sending church or designated residency churches (score –1), or are they trained in a network-directed cohort or affiliated seminary track (score +1)?

_____ Are organizational decisions for the network primarily made by the network staff and board (score +1) or by delegates from the churches (score –1)?

_____ Is support for a new church plant primarily channeled through the sending church (score –1) or through a shared network fund (score +1)?

_____ **Total**

Add up your score. If your network scored between −5 and 0, it plots on the more decentralized side of the structure continuum. If it scored between 0 and 5, your network plots on the more centralized side. The further your number is from zero, the closer your network is to one of the continuum's edges.

Plotting Your Partnership on the Network Matrix

When network leaders plot their partnership on these two continuums, it will help them clarify their network's identity, make clearer decisions, and find future partners—whether future church planters or existing church leadership teams—that are a good fit for the network. Now that you've mapped your network partnership on the alignment and structure continuums, let's talk about how the two relate.

A matrix is created when two continuums cross to create four quadrants. When we overlay the alignment and structure continuums, we have a new matrix for church networks (see the chart below). The four resulting quadrants are as follows:

- **Convictional:** centralized networks leading with theology
- **Conventional:** centralized networks aligned to a traditional and prevailing model of missions
- **Movemental:** decentralized networks leading with mission
- **Reformational:** decentralized networks leading with theology

The three networks I've served with have all been *convictional networks*—centralized partnerships that lead with theology. Each one adopted core beliefs and theological distinctives, and one now uses a common book of church order.

In the Great Commission Collective (GCC), we have required an assessment process for new church planters, trained leaders through cohorts and residencies, and maintained a central fund for new missional works.

Network Matrix

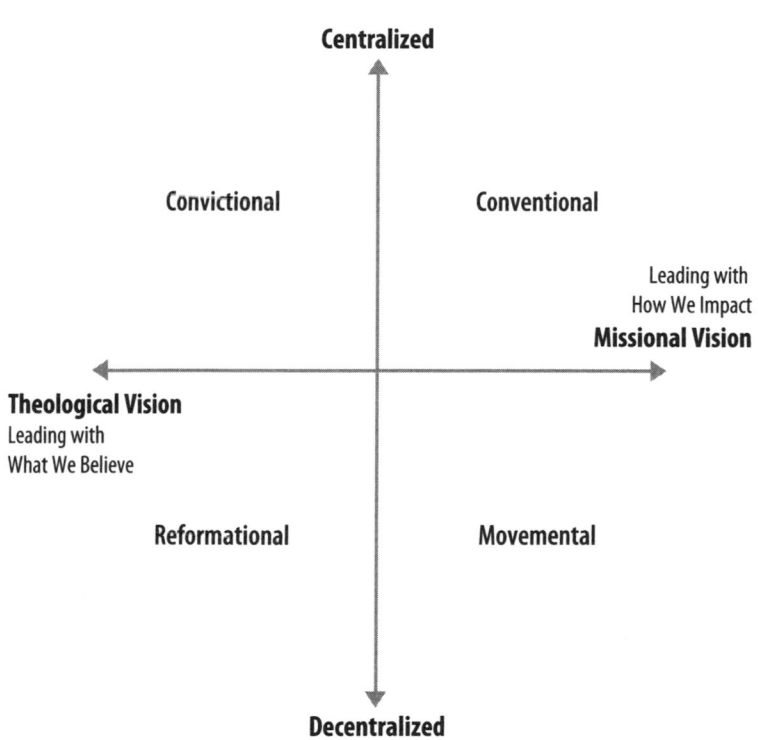

Alongside GCC, I'd also include Acts 29 and Harbor Network in the convictional network category. But it should be noted that where a network finds itself on the matrix isn't necessarily a fixed point. Think of it more as a snapshot of where they are now. A network that is in one place on the chart today could make important decisions about theological flexibility or their organizational structures that will relocate it to a different place in three years.

Large parachurch groups like Cru function as *conventional networks*—centralized partnerships that align to the prevailing model of missions. Cru has a solidly evangelical doctrinal statement, but they keep their commitments broad and work with leaders and churches from a variety of denominational backgrounds. Cru is a highly organized network with a well-defined ministry philosophy that emphasizes how evangelism and discipleship must adapt to different stages of life. As a result, two of their most recognized divisions are their campus ministry that spans to universities worldwide and their *Family Life* line of discipleship resources for married couples and parents. In the church planting world, LifeChurch.tv and the Association of Relational Churches (ARC) can be placed in the conventional networks category.

NewThing is an example of a *movemental network*, a decentralized partnership that leads with the mission. The network's website clearly states their missional purpose: "We are aligned by mission. Instead of defining ourselves by what separates us theologically, we are united by the Jesus Mission to help people find their way back to God."[3] The network's biggest goals are supporting church planting residencies and pooling financial resources to reproduce disciples, leaders, churches, and networks.

The final quadrant of the matrix is dedicated to *reformational networks*—decentralized partnerships that lead with theology. Two examples include Redeemer City to City and Vineyard USA. As with NewThing, these missional partnerships are oriented around creating multiplying church movements and not merely planting individual churches. To accomplish this purpose, power is pushed toward the edges of the movement. However, both networks are more rooted doctrinally. Redeemer City to City is an outgrowth of Redeemer Presbyterian Church, the church that Dr. Timothy Keller planted in New York City, and the network shares the church's doctrinal commitments. Similarly, Vineyard USA has clearly stated core values and beliefs that root Vineyard churches in third-wave charismatic theology.

Sweet Spots and Blind Spots

Mapping your network is an essential portion of this exercise. The continuums and categories provide some fixed points by which you can triangulate and map your location on the network matrix. But one final step remains.

The four quadrants of the Network Matrix do not exist in a vacuum. By their strengths, each network glorifies God; by their weaknesses, the networks in each quadrant struggle within the cracks of a broken world. Knowing the difference between your tribe's sweet spots and blind spots is an important step toward understanding how God's grace is already at work in your network where you need grace to work better.

What follows is a breakdown of each quadrant with a description of blind spots and sweet spots. A blind spot is an area of weakness that tends to push you toward the outer margins of your quadrant. Blind spots create imbalanced positions that undermine your network goals. Sweet spots, by contrast, help you better understand how God blesses networks in your quadrant. Regardless of your tribe, you'll be healthiest when you live in your sweet spots.

Blind Spots and Sweet Spots

The lists below are not intended to be exhaustive. They should help deepen your own discernment toward celebrating your core strengths and improving your corrupting weaknesses.

Convictional Partnerships
Centralized Networks Leading with Theology

Blind Spots
- Difficulty distinguishing between primary, secondary, and tertiary doctrines is experienced.
- Love and mercy are obscured by the priority of doctrinal discernment.
- Multiplication is bottlenecked while waiting for fully formed theological leaders.
- Bright theological borders discourage partnership outside the tribe.

Sweet Spots
- Doctrinal conviction inspires courageous leadership.
- Ministry practice is anchored in doctrinal conviction.
- High biblical literacy characterizes church leaders.
- Theological alignment fosters deeper camaraderie.

Conventional Partnerships
Centralized Networks Leading with Mission

Blind Spots
- There is less awareness of mission drift.

- These networks are more apt to franchise a brand and less apt to contextualize models.
- Organizational structures can limit expansion.
- Over time, renewal dynamics can be co-opted by stability (see chapter 4); cultural moments trigger self-preservation more than innovation.

Sweet Spots

- There is a defined ethos and process for reproduction.
- There is an ability to lead and act quickly in crisis.
- There is high quality control because of shared culture and methodology.
- Reproduction is prioritized on every organizational level.

Reformational Partnerships
Decentralized Networks Leading with Theology

Blind Spots

- Over time, theological convictions are assumed and diluted.
- It is more difficult to build and sustain community.
- Decentralization makes accountability difficult and perpetuates organizational incongruities.
- These networks are more apt to critique culture and less apt to engage culture.
- These networks lean heavily on personality to carry the message; there is a risk that teaching can become the exclusive means of transformation.
- These networks are less inclined to conduct theological triage, making unity more difficult to achieve.

Sweet Spots

- Renewal dynamics remain strong, and good news travels quickly.
- These networks are nimble and unburdened by bureaucracy.
- These networks are catalytic in leadership and attractional to outsiders.
- There is a culture of expectancy among participants.
- There is an increased capacity to broadcast the message with clarity and conviction.
- These networks often raise a prophetic voice toward the dominant culture and prevailing church models.

Movemental Partnerships
Decentralized Networks Leading with Mission

Blind Spots

- Broad metrics for success tend to be quantity driven.
- It is difficult to control and influence quality.
- Radical autonomy can grow in organization and relationships.
- Unnecessary and unintentional groups are spun off.
- Rapid multiplication leads to less rigorous discipleship and weakened DNA.
- Growth is limited by volunteer capacity.
- Leaders are evaluated by competencies, not character or theological acumen.
- Zeal for lateral growth can compromise orthodoxy and leadership maturity.

Sweet Spots

- Cycle of reproduction is simple, sustainable, and scalable.
- Organizational leadership requires less resources, finances, and management.
- There is a radical commitment to multiplication at every level—disciples, leaders, churches, and networks.
- These networks are able to adapt and innovate quickly.
- Gospel saturation is the shared outcome.

What Now?

Mapping your ministry onto the Network Matrix and then identifying some of your tribe's blind spots and sweet spots is a great start. But don't see this as the end of the exercise. Consider these five additional steps:

- **Do a team exercise.** Invite your board and elder/leadership team to map your church, network, or ministry using the Network Matrix. Discuss any surprises that surface.
- **Thank God for your sweet spots.** Talk about how God's grace was active in giving these strengths. Tell some stories about how the demonstration of these strengths has made a difference in the lives of those you serve.
- **Acknowledge where the blind spots for your quadrant apply to your group.** Be honest about where you see these weaknesses at work and where they've resulted in bad fruit. Identify two or three ways you can respond.

- **Avoid the "skinny gene" pool.** Look outside your tribe and discover whether there is another leader or group from whom you can learn. See this as an opportunity for fellowship. Humble yourself and grow from the places they are strong and you are weak. Remember, "God opposes the proud but gives grace to the humble" (James 4:6).
- **Own who you are.** The Network Matrix is not designed to move leaders into other quadrants. No, networks are typically conceived with genes that determine their identity. But knowing who you are is only the first step toward organizational health. Own who you are as a church or network and then seek to be a God-honoring, fruitful example of your quadrant.

PART

3

THE CULTURE OF PARTNERSHIP

COLLABORATION

Against Radical Individualism

What if I told you that the work of networks—the soul-enthralling summons to plant missional churches with sustainable leaders—is not a finite goal that can be completed but an unbounded call over a lifespan? In other words, there is no threshold we'll cross after which we'll be able to suddenly shout, "Nailed it! Our work is finally done." In fact, even when our time is over, the work goes on.

Imagine what we do in church planting networks as a game.[1] Most games are bounded. They have fixed rules, a defined way of winning, and a clear beginning, middle, and end. When the clock hits zero, a bounded game is over and we crown the champion.

An unbounded game, by contrast, is more dynamic. There's no final whistle or finish line. Unbounded games don't have winners; they have teams that measure their success by their ability to keep playing. Monopoly and football are bounded games; marriage and friendship are unbounded ones. When you're playing an unbounded game, you can't go it alone; such games call for teamwork, perseverance, and a vision for the future.

In this chapter, I want to help you see that God has designed the ministries of discipleship and multiplication as unbounded games. They are not competitions but shared investments in the next generation. When you frame your service in a network as an unbounded journey, the infinite scope awakens within you an urgency for our next virtue—namely, *collaboration*.

> *God has designed the ministries of discipleship and multiplication as unbounded games. They are not competitions but shared investments in the next generation.*

Collaboration: Solve for X

In chapter 1, we explored the biblical call to interdependence. But while interdependence is the foundation for collaboration, the terms are not synonymous. If interdependence is the conviction, collaboration is the practice. Interdependence says, "We need each other." Collaboration says, "Let's accomplish something together. Let's create and make something together to solve for X."

Collaboration is more than a trendy leadership virtue drawn from Fortune 500 companies; it's an expression of what it means to be human. Humans were created as social beings. Genesis tells us that Adam was incomplete until Eve arrived (Genesis 2:18). Then when the woman joined him, they were commissioned to work together to fill the earth and subdue it (Genesis 1:28–30).

But collaboration is not just about the creation mandate. The New Testament makes clear that it's for Great Commission work as well. Paul tells us that God set up the church in such a way that we're pushed toward one another: "The eye cannot say to the hand, 'I have no need of you,' nor again the head to the feet, 'I have no need of you'" (1 Corinthians 12:21). Each member of the local church needs the other members, and the same is true beyond the local body. Pastors need a network beyond their local elder team. And networks need kingdom help from groups beyond their tribe.

It may feel counterintuitive at first—especially for those of us who hated group work in school—but God has designed the mission so that it moves forward through the synergy of *we*. In the unbounded Great Commission game, churches can achieve together what no one church can accomplish alone. As the African proverb says, "If you want to go fast, go alone. If you want to go far, *go together*."[2]

> *God has designed the mission so that it moves forward through the synergy of we.*

So how can we measure the health and quality of our collaboration? How do we know if our shared and unbounded work as a network is making a difference in the life of our churches? Here are three ways:

First, healthy collaboration finds inspiration in sharing models. In Paul's letters, we see him celebrating the work of God in one church to provoke faith in another group of believers (2 Corinthians 9:1–2; 1 Thessalonians 1:6–8). Knowing that his letter to the Colossians would also be read to the Laodiceans, Paul celebrated the example of faith and love the Colossians had for one another (Colossians 1:3–4). He used the Thessalonians and, lo and behold, even the Corinthians—bet you didn't expect that twist—as examples for the Macedonians! Paul regularly referenced the lives and examples of individual believers as well. To Paul, inspiration was an essential benefit of collaboration.

This means a lot to me. I can't count the number of times I've been personally inspired by hearing about how another congregation is doing—how they're living on mission, caring for one another, reaching their city, innovating new ideas, or just generally reflecting God's glory. It stirs my faith to see the example of others. I think we're all wired that way.

Sharing models is the way to wisdom. The high-tech world has a principle called Joy's Law. Sun Microsystems cofounder Bill Joy famously discovered that the knowledge his team needed for progress couldn't be found in a singular genius or even in a one-on-one connection. In fact, Joy believed that the wisdom his team needed would often be found outside the borders of his organization. Joy would tell his team, "No matter who you are, most of the smartest people work for someone else."[3]

Now honestly, I'm not sure vocalizing that is the best way to mobilize your team, but the principle underneath Joy's words is where we need to focus. It's no different in churches and church planting networks. One of God's goals for extra-local partnerships is that greater ministry is stoked as individual churches' strengths are celebrated and used to bring joyful encouragement to the larger church. God often places the wisdom we need outside of ourselves, sometimes even outside of our teams. This strategy makes us dependent on God and keeps the church (and churches) moving toward one another.

This means that whenever pastors get together with other church leaders, a pastor should expect to be challenged by what they see and hear. Through network collaboration, every church's culture, systems, structures, and strategies can be evaluated under the light of more mature church models and leaders who have been schooled longer in the grammar of gospel. Large urban churches can even take a fresh look at what small or rural churches can teach them. The small church may not have much to say about how to scale a church program or staff, but the larger church may find a wealth of wisdom on contextualized ministry, personal evangelism, and training lay elders. Once you get collaboration, you see the principle applying in every direction.

If we're going to experience corporate renewal and be challenged to innovate for the sake of the mission, we must learn from and collaborate with those who are outside of our immediate circle. After all, shared pain is pain halved, and shared ideas are ideas multiplied.

Second, healthy collaboration generously shares resources. If a network is going to grow, churches and leaders must share their resources. They must make reciprocal sacrifices for the sake of the mission. Just consider the cost that the Philippians paid when they sent Epaphroditus to minister to Paul's needs (Philippians 2:25–30).

Epaphroditus was deeply loved by the Philippians. Yet despite his remarkable qualities, the Philippians gave him up. Joining Paul was not a trip to Disney World; the young man put his life at risk for Paul (Philippians 2:27, 30). Then Paul— the guy running his ministry from a prison cell—eventually surrendered Epaphroditus and sent him back to the Philippians. Why? Because he was convinced that doing so would better serve the church (2:25).

Paul's entire relationship with the Philippians was characterized by this sort of fruitful reciprocity and resource sharing. It wasn't just their sending Epaphroditus back and forth. I'd be remiss if I didn't mention the unique role the Philippians had in supporting Paul's extra-local ministry financially as well.

As we saw in chapter 1, the Philippian church was strong. They had solid elders and deacons (1:1), a reputation for obedience (2:12), and a well-established history of support (4:15–16). In the panoply of churches that partnered together, the Philippians were among the most mature. If a case could be made for any New Testament church growing beyond their need for interdependence, collaboration, and teamwork, it was the church in Philippi.

But that's not what happened. The strength of the Philippian church produced *more* support for Paul and his team. This church collaborated *more* with other churches in the Pauline network. In response, Paul also considered how his helpers could be of strategic support to the Philippians (2:19–30). And the Philippian church became an example of how maturity fuels not autonomy but reciprocity (4:14–18).

A maturing church member wouldn't say, "Now that I've grown, I need my pastors less!" No, the member may need his pastors differently, but they are still needed. Moreover, if the member is maturing, the pastors also need that person. Maturity delivers the member into *service*, not independence.[4] The same is true in a network.

Healthy collaboration involves large-souled mutuality, the kind of partnership we inhabit together when we can both serve and be served. The network's work to plant and serve churches is only possible when local churches see the value of reciprocity, respond to the network's vision, and willingly say, "We love partnership, and we want to invest more."

> *Healthy collaboration involves large-souled mutuality, the kind of partnership we inhabit together when we can both serve and be served.*

Third, healthy collaboration invests in the next generation. For networks to be effective, the pastors and leaders within the network must have sharp eyes to see future leaders. Moreover, they must be forward-thinking enough to train them.

When Paul wrote to the Philippians, he gave Timothy the strongest of commendations: "I have no one like him who will be genuinely concerned for your welfare" (Philippians 2:20). This is a remarkable statement when we consider where Timothy started.

Timothy's father was Greek, and his mother was Jewish. He grew up with the complexities of being a mixed-race kid. We know about the faithfulness of Eunice and Lois, Timothy's mother and grandmother (2 Timothy 1:5), but Timothy still remained uncircumcised long into his adulthood (Acts 16:3). That fact signifies the tension he must have faced as he lived under the authority of his unbelieving Greek dad.

Timothy also had a reputation of being a weak and fearful soul. Humanly speaking, he was hopelessly unfit to assume the weighty responsibilities of pastoral leadership. John R. W. Stott describes Timothy as "naturally shy . . . young in years, frail in physique, retiring in disposition."[5]

I love Timothy's story, because it reminds me of my own. There was a time when I was the next generation. At the age of thirty, I was wading into the complex world of network leadership, and I knew practically nothing save the fact that our growing network was desperate enough to recruit me. I'll never forget the older men who overlooked my immaturity and invested in my training. They believed in Paul's unbounded, multigenerational vision: "What you have heard from me in the presence of many witnesses entrust to faithful men, who will be able to teach others also" (2 Timothy 2:2).

In the Great Commission Collective, we aim at helping church leaders through five different levels of training. It begins with (1) local discipleship, which leads to (2) an intentional leadership pipeline. For those who are called, we provide (3) church planter training and (4) ongoing support while each church plant gets off the ground. The final level is (5) helping churches start city and regional church planting networks. We want to program this way because we believe that healthy collaboration elevates training.

We also know that for the mission to go forward into the

future, we've got to take risks on people. Young Timothy may have been a youthful lamb, but when the gospel took hold of him, he became a lion of the faith. Paul later wrote, "You know Timothy's proven worth, how as a son with a father he has served with me in the gospel" (Philippians 2:22). Timothy would later become bishop of the Ephesian church, a man who exercised enormous influence until AD 97 when he was martyred while pleading with an angry mob to renounce their vain worship and flee for salvation to the risen Savior.

Paul's unbounded mindset outlasted him through Timothy. And though Paul, Timothy, and countless other martyrs were killed for their faith, the unbounded work of Great Commission collaboration goes on.

Beware the Vice: Radical Individualism

It's mission-critical that we understand the difference between a bounded and an unbounded mindset. Mixing them up can be disastrous. If two people think of their marriage as a competition and one declares themselves to be the victor, a discerning eye immediately sees that they have lost.

Sadly, pastors and network leaders tend to borrow our leadership models from misdirected business leaders who mistakenly talk like they're playing bounded games. Such leaders talk of victory, owning their competition, and achieving dominance through their market share. The vice that leads them to play a bounded game is *radical individualism.*

Most organisms and organizations experience a natural progression toward healthy independence and autonomy, which isn't a bad thing. People need to grow in self-awareness and differentiate themselves as individuals within healthy communities. Birds learn to fly and leave the nest. Kids leave home and go to college or the workplace. In the world of multichurch, many multisite campuses have now spun off from their mother churches to become full-fledged, independent entities. In such cases, greater autonomy has become a milestone in a journey toward healthy maturity.

But the problem with a bounded mindset is that it can radicalize this tendency. In the opening chapters of Carl Trueman's masterwork *The Rise and Triumph of the Modern Self*, he explains that most people throughout history have understood themselves in connection to others; they've seen themselves in view of their place in society.[6] A political man finds his identity in the contributions he makes to public life, a businessman in producing excellent goods or services, and a religious man in service to God and the church.[7] The point, according to Trueman, is that institutions angled us away from ourselves and toward the community—toward unbounded service and collaboration.

But today, particularly in the Western world, a seismic shift has occurred, creating a fault line beneath the surface of societal relationships. Today, people are predisposed to compete, and institutions are expected to serve each person's quest for personal happiness, inner peace, and the drive to win.[8] The individualism vice makes self-centeredness our default setting, and when this vice goes undetected, unity and community can be corrupted altogether.

> *Today, people are predisposed to compete, and institutions are expected to serve each person's quest for personal happiness, inner peace, and drive to win.*

It's been this way since the beginning of time. Adam and Eve's bite of the fruit introduced a godless individualism into our genetics (Genesis 3:6–7; Romans 5:12). In Adam, our internal GPS was skewed by sin. Our sense of self no longer triangulates its position from God and others. Instead, we hide from God and throw others under the bus (Genesis 3:12).

The sad news is that we don't just find the radical self *out there* in society. It's often just as rampant in the church, waging war against personal sacrifice and communal commitments. An individualistic person refuses to subject themselves to group norms, and they won't receive help from others. They see network leadership as barely tolerable. After all, if you've prioritized the self as your noblest pursuit—and wisdom, direction, and authority all come from within—it's hard to imagine anyone more qualified to lead than you.

> *If you've prioritized the self as your noblest pursuit—and wisdom, direction, and authority all come from within—it's hard to imagine anyone more qualified to lead than you.*

In our radically autonomous culture, leaders—whether they are serving churches, neighborhood associations, clubs, or even sports teams—must be aware of this temptation. Collaboration dies when no one is permitted to challenge the absolute priority of the individual leader. Partnership dies when serving others is trumped by self-interest and personal gain.

The pastor who believes it is a *right* for them to be alone or a *right* for their church to be alone is a pastor on the road to disaster. Few things are more dangerous to cohesiveness than when the individualistic and ungrounded self goes viral. Its tongue begins to speak the language of emancipation,[9] and it breaks free from family, cultural, organizational, and institutional expectations. Self-destiny and self-determinism are the unexamined impulses behind this unshackling. Freedom means the absence of rules, restraints, and commitments. When the ravenous *Me* moves to the center, communities lose their ability to find common ground. The key question for life becomes, "What can I do to make myself happy?"

Vice Audit 3: Radical Individualism

Rank the degree to which you agree with the following statements on a scale of 1–5 (5 = strongly agree, 4 = agree, 3 = neutral, 2 = disagree, 1 = strongly disagree). Write your ranking in the blank to the left of each statement.

_____ 1. Our church's leaders are more predisposed to seeing other churches in our region or network as competitors than we are to serving the other churches for the greater good.

_____ 2. Leaders in our church typically buck against the group norms of our network. It's hard to find common ground with other churches and leaders.

_____ 3. It's hard for our leaders to recognize there are others outside our church who can help us.

_____ 4. It's difficult for the leaders at our church to imagine a definition of success that's different from the way we've always defined it.

_____ 5. Our church leadership team struggles to make commitments to outside groups, particularly if that commitment involves a level of sacrifice.

_____ **Total**

If your church and leadership scored between 0–8, you are likely strong collaborators. If you scored between 9–18, take some time to sit with your leadership team and talk through the three expressions of healthy collaboration discussed in this chapter. If you scored between 19–25, your church is in danger of succumbing to the vice of radical individualism. Take some time to confess this to the Lord and begin praying that God will help you develop a church culture that looks away from "Me" and more to "We."

Do you see how destructive radical individualism can be? By appealing to the basest of our desires—to be first, to be best, to be preferred, to be considered great, to win—unfettered individualism corrupts community, demeans society, and destroys collaboration. The wise church leader—whether the church is independent or connected with a denominational structure—must accept that they need autonomy sufficient to exercise their role but not so much that it obscures their need.

Fighting Individualism by Locking Arms Together on Mission

As the Second World War began, experts projected that as many as four million people in England would experience a psychological breakdown during the air raids. But even as people died in their homes and neighborhoods while doing mundane daily chores, an extraordinary phenomenon occurred:

As the Blitz progressed, psychiatric hospitals around the country saw admissions go *down*. Emergency services in London reported an average of only two cases of "bomb neuroses" a week. Psychiatrists watched in puzzlement as long-standing patients saw their symptoms subside during the period of intense air raids. Voluntary admissions to psychiatric wards noticeably declined, and even epileptics reported having fewer seizures. "Chronic neurotics of peacetime now drive ambulances," one doctor remarked. Another ventured to suggest that some people actually did *better* during wartime.[10]

Why does war have a positive effect on mental health? It's because the people involved in the conflicts encounter a compelling summons to meet an aching need. As a result, factors that normally would shake or divide them are made temporarily meaningless.

Sometimes it takes a war to shake us out of our neurosis and remind us that there's more to life than what orbits around ourselves. But what happened during the Blitz illustrates a reality that is just as true in peacetime as it is in warfare. Commitment and collaboration are central to society's health. They're fundamental to what it means to be healthy image bearers who are created for eternity.

The truth is that networks also flourish when leaders respond to a compelling summons and meet an aching need. There may be some injustices, some gaping hole in the church, some church planting dream or gospel call that grip the heart. There may be a new model that excites us, or a young leader on whom we want to take a risk. Sometimes our hearts are captured by the biblical model of interdependence. Sometimes we simply discover the difficulty of doing it alone. Such experiences can spark a desire within us to find like-minded people with whom we can share reciprocally for the sake of a greater good.

A network does a lot of things. It may offer training, assess church planters, provide coaching for pastors and staff, put on events or conferences, or help local churches navigate times of crisis. But the one thing a network must never do is become an end for those in it. We must aim for something much bigger, something that nurtures a more soul-satisfying fruit.

If interdependence is our *conviction*, and humble *collaboration* —interdependence applied—is our *practice*, then a gospel *culture* will be the result. This is what I will explore in the rest of this section.

Cultivating Gospel Culture

"Culture," says Andy Crouch, "is what human beings make of the world."[11] Radical individualism is what we make of ourselves. It's culture making inverted. When imagination bends inward, we see a world made only for our own image. But the gospel unshackles culture making, inspiring souls that radiate with the boundless beauty of Christ's love. If network leaders want to create the latter, then the creative work we do—the programs, art, books, events, and training to which we dedicate our time—can't be designed as fame-grabbing, Nebuchadnezzar-style monuments to ourselves. A healthy gospel culture doesn't seek to draw attention to individual platforms. It doesn't build churches that exist in isolation from one another or for their own glory. And it doesn't play a bounded, competitive, and individualistic game that panders to rivalry and self-interest.

No, God has called us instead to an unbounded vision that sees the eternal picture. Through networks, we create spaces for church leaders to lift their gaze to gospel realities and serve one another. In our events and trainings, and even more importantly in our collaborative work and friendships, we're imagining what church multiplication and leadership longevity might make of the world. In service to the King, we're cultivating those unbounded dreams together.

This is how we'll defeat the spirit of radical autonomy. Hyperindividualist people believe that satisfaction can only be achieved by making themselves strong and accumulating all they want. But the flourishing life described in the Bible cannot be lived with *Me* at the center. We are called to an unbounded, self-sacrificing life grounded in a bloody death. As B. B. Warfield wrote:

> Self-sacrifice brought Christ into the world. And self-sacrifice will lead us, His followers, not away from but into the midst of men. Wherever men suffer, there will we be to comfort. Wherever men strive, there will we be to help. Wherever men fail, there will we be to uplift. Wherever men succeed, there will we be to rejoice.[12]

That's it. The only vaccination against the viral strain of radical individualism is to leverage your whole being for connection and service outside of yourself. That's the only way that *We*, as people created for the glory of God in community, can flourish in a fallen world.

As I wrote in chapter 1, conversion begins with a "God and me" experience, but when we embrace the other-centered nature of the gospel, we move out toward others. It's true for individual Christians, and it's true for churches as well. Just as Christians who experience renewal seek relationships for service and connection, so also churches that experience renewal seek affiliation. They seek to unite their lives and resources as a blessing to other churches and the world.

The only vaccination against the viral strain of radical autonomy is to leverage your whole being for connection and service outside of yourself.

Jesus tells us that if we want to be great, we must be servants (Mark 9:35). If we desire to be treated in a particular way, we should do to others as we would have them do to us (Luke 6:31). We must not merely consider our own interests but also the interests of others (Philippians 2:4). Embedded in the gospel is the glorious news that we live for something larger than ourselves.

As cultural commentator David Brooks observes, "A commitment to community involves moving from 'I' stories to 'We' stories. The move, as always is downward and then outward. Down into ourselves in vulnerability and then outward in solidarity with others."[13] A commitment to living as a committed network begins with admitting our need, beholding Christ's forgiveness, and then responding to his good news by locking arms together as we go on mission.

When this happens—when a leader or church begins to see the kingdom beyond themselves—you know the gospel is at work. Such churches believe, "The mission is bigger than our church; our field is bigger than our tribe." And with a new outward posture, collaboration finds purchase and begins to grow. Networks find new meaning for their existence. And churches connect to do gospel work, all for the glory of God.

THE DYNAMICS
OF RENEWAL

Against Institutionalism

You've probably heard of Washington Irving's 1819 legend of Rip Van Winkle. In the story, the protagonist, Rip, is a good-natured but lazy man who hikes into the Catskill Mountains to escape his shrewish wife. On his journey, Van Winkle meets a magical dwarf who invites him to an all-night kegger. During the roaring celebration, Rip drinks from a flagon of enchanted schnapps that sends him straight into a twenty-year sleep.

When Rip left his New York home, he passed a portrait of King George III hanging above the local tavern. Upon Rip's return, the face on the sign had changed to that of George Washington.[1] That tavern sign forms a subtle feature of Irving's tale, but as Martin Luther King Jr. would later observe, it represents a poignant truth.[2] Rip had not only snoozed for twenty years, and it wasn't just that his hair was gray and his face creased with wrinkles. Van Winkle had slept through a revolution. The world had undergone a cataclysmic change while he remained fast asleep.

We've been looking at the virtues and vices that make the

difference between fulfillment and failure in church partnerships. The truth is that on the beaches of every network or denomination, there is always some revolution coming ashore. There are small skirmishes and raging battles that determine whether networks are fossilizing or flourishing. Wise leaders do not shut their eyes to these realities. If we do, enemy invasions can occur while we sleep, and we'll awaken to discover we've missed the revolution.

Beware the Vice: Institutionalism

Years ago, I read Alonzo McDonald's chapter in the book *No God But God*.[3] There he makes a passing reference to the life cycle of a "work of God," describing the subtle changes and tectonic shifts through which most organizations progress. We can label this life cycle with five *Ms*—minister, ministry, movement, machine, and monument.

Gospel movements typically begin with an individual *minister* whom God calls and to whom he gives a compelling vision. Like a tractor beam, people are drawn to that leader. They cluster together until the individual multiplies himself—the minister becomes a *ministry*; the person becomes a people, and a unifying cause inspires and coalesces their energy. The people's synergy kindles a *movement*—a fresh, prophetic, and future-oriented work that sparks a vision for sacrificial ministry.

Funny thing about movements: As growth comes and time passes, an inexorable need to organize occurs. Authority must be mapped, beliefs defined, culture codified—vital steps toward institutionalizing must be taken to protect the quality and sustainability of the movement. When led wisely, key renewal dynamics are preserved. But when leaders are asleep at the wheel, the institutionalizing sets a collision course for the shoals of *institutionalism*.

Institutionalism occurs whenever a ministry or organization begins to exist more for those it employs than for those it serves. This is the *machine* stage. Abraham Kuyper once called the church an "organized organism;"[4] the machine stage is where the organic begins to get organized right out of ministry; mechanization begins to devour dynamic life.

At this stage, ministry becomes an end rather than a means. Brian Sanders once observed that large organizations seem to have immune systems that attack growth and innovation. "Sometimes this process is malicious and premeditated, but most of the time, it's unconscious," he writes. "It is simply the nature of an existing system to preserve its operating model."[5] As this happens, the wet cement of institutionalism begins to harden, and the movement forms into a mere mechanism. Polity and policy exert supremacy over the movement dynamics that once energized the cause.

This sets the stage for the final *M*. When the machine runs too long without the fuel of renewal, what was once a movement becomes a mere *monument*—a shrine to a former period in the organization's life, fit only to be eulogized by those who remember its history.

Don't misunderstand me. The question is not whether a movement will institutionalize; the question is whether it will do so wisely. Like people, organizations age. The older we get, the more we need to organize to truly flourish. Childless married couples in the church often advocate for unscheduled, free-spirited community. Then the kids arrive! Couples quickly learn that for community to continue, it will need to be organized and scheduled right alongside naps, feedings, playdates . . . and even sex.

Age draws us toward institutionalizing. Whether it's homes, churches, governments, or freedoms, each must be carefully organized and protected so that civilization flourishes. Now, in this discussion, words matter. The pursuit of organization and institutionalizing does not automatically trigger the vice of *institutionalism*. Systems do not automatically send us from movement to machine. No, that shift usually occurs as the result of one or more forms of movement glaucoma.

The Symptoms of Movement Glaucoma

Ten years ago, I was diagnosed with glaucoma—an eye disease that unconsciously darkens one's field of vision. It attacks the center point of vision while leaving the periphery relatively unaffected. People with glaucoma can miss the middle and focus on the fringe.

Leaders do this too. We suffer from various forms of organizational glaucoma. We stare straight ahead, believing we are focused on the center. But our visual field is darkened in the middle, so what we are beholding most clearly is what is on the margins.

Here are symptoms of movement glaucoma that appear when an organization begins to drift toward institutionalism:

Symptom #1: Tension blindness. We know we've moved toward institutionalism when we are unable to see the organizational tensions that exist within partnerships. When this happens,

- custom consumes vision;
- security overshadows sacrifice;
- tenure displaces talent;
- rules replace relationships;

- centralization sidelines collaboration; and
- maintenance usurps the mission.

On the one hand, we must not be tempted to think that customs and rules, security and tenure, or centralization and maintenance are evils in and of themselves. They are not. The pairs I've listed above do not represent opposing poles of right and wrong but rather the normal push and pull between institutional and movement dynamics.

In the "Mapping Your Network" section in part 2, I wrote about key partnership tensions that can be mapped along an alignment continuum and a structure continuum. I named two of the quadrants in the resulting Network Matrix "institutional" and "movemental." I want to make clear that in critiquing institutionalism in this chapter, I'm not taking a backhanded swipe at networks that plot themselves in the institutional category, nor am I giving special props to those in the movemental quadrant. After all, as I've already indicated, the networks where I've served would all be classified as convictional, not as institutional or movemental.

Even though the terminology is similar, my aim is different in this chapter. I'm thinking here of central tensions that network and church leaders in every category must live in. As Tim Keller has written, "Organizations should have both institutional characteristics and movement dynamics."[6] Both are good and necessary for a growing church or network.

Prudent leaders live self-consciously within the gravitational field of each tension. They avoid hyperspiritualizing one pole over another or climbing one side to perch on the moral high ground. For example, it is appropriate for a church or network to shop for the best insurance plan. It's essential for an organization to have clear structures for accountability. And it's wise to have a plan for maintaining the facilities and developing the staff. To refuse these organizational characteristics is to lose vitality and fragment the team.

As missiologist Roland Allen once observed, "Our love of organization leads us to rely upon it."[7] When this happens, form replaces faith. Means become ends. And our delights shift from the treasures of Christ to the traction of organizational clarity. That's why the best leadership organizes in such a way that vision and mission, collaboration and relationships, talent, and sacrifice all endure as part of our institutional character. If we're not aware of the need to occupy these tensions—if we're not intentional about protecting the dynamics of gospel movement—the creep of institutionalism will choke the life right out of our networks.

When leaders aren't diligent to push against it, our churches and networks will float toward comfort, convention, conformity—the machinery of institutionalism. Rather than being *ecclesia reformata, semper reformanda* (the church reformed, always reforming), we embody Newton's law of inertia. We're objects at rest that stay at rest—like Rip Van Winkle for twenty years. Gospel mission requires a studied awareness of our natural tendency followed by an intentional effort to reverse it. We must deny institutional comfort and create momentum that moves us toward mission.

> **When leaders aren't diligent to push in the opposite direction, our churches and networks will float toward comfort, convention, conformity— the machinery of institutionalism.**

Symptom #2: Rigidity blindness. Preventing leadership glaucoma means managing the changes that attend the growth and maturity of your church or network. When I was a young leader, this was much easier. I thrived on the challenge of bringing gospel clarity to chaos. But as I've grown older and more comfortable, I'm tempted to make my preferences into principles and my methods immutable. You get it. As we age, we become entrenched in our way of doing things—the *right* way of doing things. But our high points are all in the past.

I remember visiting a restaurant that had a killer review from a food critic posted by the cash register for all to see; the trouble was that the review was decades old. Bono nails the rigidity blindness symptom when he sings, "You've got stuck in a moment, and you can't get out of it."[8] The trouble is that locking into the past makes us inflexible in the present.

I sometimes use the phrase *dictionary leadership* to describe those who are tempted toward rigidity blindness. A dictionary defines. It removes ambiguity and enhances clarity. Dictionary leaders strive for clear definition as a way of understanding God's will. That's not a bad thing. After all, the New Testament calls leaders to teach not just doctrine, but *sound* doctrine (Titus 2:1). We must define to distinguish bad ideas from biblical ones, to divide truth from error. So far so good.

But dictionary leaders can become paralyzed in the absence of clear definitions or prescribed pathways. Ministry unfolds in a world where God will frustrate our best efforts to simplify in order to form and shape us. God often acts to remind leaders that he is infinitely larger than our categories. He defies definition. "His understanding," says Isaiah, "is unsearchable" (Isaiah 40:28). Moreover, some of his best soul work happens when we're escorted beyond what our theories of life and leadership can imagine.

In a fallen world, mystery is baked into life and leadership. We suffer. People disappoint us. Satan seduces a member of our team, and we're left reeling. When the worst happens, a dictionary leader can be left in places where clarity and definition don't come. In fact, a leader dependent on clarity and outcomes can, in a time of suffering, become shipwrecked on the shoals of ambiguity. They find it difficult to rest under the dark clouds of mystery when a torrent of unanswered questions overwhelms the soul.

And it's not just suffering. Anyone who has planted a church can tell you that in the melee of mission, church planting and network leadership will deliver us to places that challenge our definitions and expectations. Certainly, there are times when we need the dictionary. But the mystery, adventure, and complexities of mission are better explored with a different approach. Let's call it *thesaurus leadership.*

A thesaurus supplies synonyms—different words that mean the same thing. Thesaurus leaders don't eschew definition, but they're willing to explore optional ways of pursuing the same path. Not all thesaurus leaders thrive on change, but they recognize how essential it is to anticipate and adapt to it. They recognize that the gospel goes into a variety of contexts, and they're eager to pursue an assortment of tools and a range of possibilities to get it there. Thesaurus leaders aren't afraid to adopt a broad vocabulary for talking about life in a broken world, and they're happy to imagine different ways the gospel may move forward—as long as the gospel core remains unchanged. To paraphrase Evelyn Underhill, they know if God was tiny enough to be tweetable, he would not be large enough to be praised.[9]

When churches leave, suffering arrives, or the anomalies of ministry crash the network party, thesaurus leaders have a broader vocabulary through which to explore options and discuss necessary audibles. Thesaurus leaders call for clarity, but they do not idolize it. Unrelenting ambiguity becomes an opportunity to entrust all we don't know to the One who knows all.

Are you seeing either of these symptoms in your life? Are you aware of the tensions that organizational leadership requires? Or are you organizing the life right out of your organization? Are you embracing the contextual impulse of a thesaurus leader, or are you tempted to define your mission or ministry models so narrowly that they are unable to be replicated in new contexts?

> *Thesaurus leaders aren't afraid to adopt a broad vocabulary for talking about life in a broken world, and they're happy to imagine different ways the gospel may move forward— as long as the gospel core remains unchanged.*

The answer for institutionalism is not ignoring organizational development and institutional needs. No, we must dwell within these tensions. The answer to institutionalism begins with an awareness that our impulse to narrowly define and rigidly organize might be killing our ministry. That impulse may offer evidence that we've started to believe that the real power is found in systems and control rather than in the transforming power of the gospel.

Vice Audit 4: Institutionalism

Rank the degree to which you agree with the following statements on a scale of 1-5 (5 = strongly agree, 4 = agree, 3 = neutral, 2 = disagree, 1 = strongly disagree). Write your ranking in the blank to the left of each statement.

_____ 1. Our team craves clarity in a way that diminishes our willingness to take risks for the mission.

_____ 2. We're tempted to turn our preferences into immutable principles.

_____ 3. Our team trends toward dictionary leadership, not thesaurus leadership. In our organization, we regularly judge new ideas by whether they fit with our preconceived definitions, custom, and rules.

_____ 4. It's not common for leaders on our team to confess their sins to others in the organization.

_____ 5. Our team spends more time on maintaining ministry agendas and programs than we do pursing a culture of creative multiplication.

_____ **Total**

If your church and leadership scored between 0–8, you have the kind of culture that is positioned for movement. If you scored between 9–18, take some time to sit with your leadership team and talk through the dynamics of personal and organizational renewal in the chapter. If you scored between 19–25, your church is in danger of succumbing to the vice of institutionalism. Take some time to confess this to the Lord and begin praying that he will help you develop a church culture that embodies movement dynamics.

The Dynamics of Personal Renewal

When the gravitational pull of institutionalism is strong, what should we do? What steps should we take if our ministry already seems like a machine grinding slowly to a halt?

The book of Judges offers some helpful insights. The book is organized around cycles of decline and renewal in Israel. Interestingly, a repeating pattern surfaces in chapter 2. First, God's people forsake him (2:11–13). Then God disciplines them through foreign oppression (vv. 14–15). Third, God is moved to compassion as the people cry out to him in distress (v. 18). Finally, God answers their prayer by raising up a judge to deliver them (2:16). The book of Judges is man → movement → monument, rinse and repeat.

Now don't miss the connection back to our second partnership virtue. The instruments of God's renewal are *individual leaders*. As Richard Lovelace says,

> It appears that a general principle concerning the deliverance of God's people is being hinted at here: redemption comes under the direction of leaders whom God raises up in his sovereign mercy in response to the deep longing and intercession of the laity generated under the pressure of defeat or suffering.[10]

Lovelace goes on to say that "the renewal periods in Judges usually spanned forty years, the lifetime of the human leader."[11] What do we learn from this? If you are reading this as a leader in a ministry where people are praying for renewal, what steps should you take?

Here's the thing. Renewal doesn't begin with a church or network; it begins with bold strokes of leadership that push the group from ingrown to outward. If you're a leader, you must believe that renewal is first about *you*. It begins with three personal postures: looking *back*, looking *up*, looking *out*. Let's unpack each one.

Looking back means remembering the gospel. When we look back, we're acknowledging that the power to persevere in ministry does not come from within ourselves but from the work that Christ has done outside of us in his death and resurrection. The primal power that converted is the same power that renews and changes us—the gospel of Jesus Christ. A gospel movement must not leave his good news behind. We must go back to it again and again. In the New Testament, churches flourished because the dynamic power of the gospel was at work trans-forming individuals. Indeed, says Paul, "in the whole world it is bearing fruit and increasing" (Colossians 1:6).

The primal power that converted is the same power that renews and changes us—the gospel of Jesus Christ. A gospel movement must not leave his good news behind.

You see, the gospel is not a stagnant body of information but an uncontain-able message that grows and produces fruit in those who embrace and apply it. In Romans 1:16, Paul calls it "the power of God for salvation." In other words, the message of the gospel empowers the transformation it calls for—in both believers and unbelievers. Charles Spurgeon once compared the gospel to a lion. He wrote:

> Suppose a number of persons were to take it into their heads that they had to defend a lion, a full-grown king of beasts! There he is in the cage, and here come all the soldiers of the army to fight for him. Well, I should suggest to them, if they would not object, and feel that it was humbling to them, that they should kindly stand back, and open the door, and let the lion out! I believe that would be the best way of defending him, for he would take care of himself; and the best "apology" for the gospel is to let the gospel out. Never mind about defending Deuteronomy or the whole of the Pentateuch; preach Jesus Christ and him crucified. Let the Lion out and see who will dare to approach him. The Lion of the tribe of Judah will soon drive away all his adversaries.[12]

Looking back means opening the cage door and letting the gospel do its work. Preach it to yourself. Thank God for the gospel. Swap stories about the impact of the gospel. Renewal comes when the gospel is recovered, treasured, and embraced.

Looking up means prayer. When you remember the good news, it sends you in a clear direction—to your knees! Prayer is our declaration of dependence on God to do the work of God. It's an admission that renewal springs from Christ's gospel work within us and not something we can manufacture on our own.

Prayer does not return us to a leadership skill or organizational expertise. Rather, it returns us to the power and presence of Christ himself. Jesus is the source of our renewal. It springs from waiting on him. "They who wait for the LORD shall renew their strength" (Isaiah 40:31). Prayer acknowledges this reality, and it puts us in the posture of Mary rather than in the posture of Martha. It keeps us sitting at the feet of Jesus and listening to him instead of merely expending energy to create the illusion of progress. Looking up reminds us that renewal is not a ministry device we wield or a transactional arrangement we negotiate, but instead renewal is rooted in a relationship with our Savior. Renewal is experienced in spending time with him and hearing his voice.

Looking out is the final personal posture, aimed at both the heart and mind. When we look up to God, we discover that he is sending us out to others. His activity does not terminate with us. No, in Great Commission fashion, our missionary God sends us out to multiply disciples. And when we're looking out to others, the benefits are bountiful. We're connected to folks who think differently, even innovatively, about the churches and partnerships we are building. Looking out is also a way to walk in the footsteps of the Savior.

After all, tax collectors, prostitutes, and fishermen were not the cultural icons of the first century. But Jesus was a friend of those sinners (Matthew 11:19; Luke 7:34). In the incarnation, the Son not only moved away from the glories of heaven to take on human flesh, but he also moved to the edges of society. Jesus associated with the marginal. He listened to them. He loved them. Jesus made them feel welcome in his presence. The gospel became real because it was embodied by someone who brought outsiders into his life.

Going to the margins improves our leadership glaucoma, and it's life-giving. You see, the roles we occupy in the Christian ministry too easily keep us in a bubble. Unintentionally, we become insulated, living in an echo chamber of affirmation with others who think just like us. If you have been a Christian leader for a while, you know the tendency to spend more time with other leaders, or with mature believers, or just with people who mitigate their perspectives because they derive some gain from our approval. It's good to "equip the saints for the work of ministry" (Ephesians 4:12), but if we're not also doing "the work of an evangelist" (2 Timothy 4:5), our perspective on people and how they think will become distorted.

> *If you have been a Christian leader for a while then you know the tendency to spend more time with other leaders, or with mature believers, or just with people who mitigate their perspectives because they derive some gain from our approval.*

Bubbles bend reality. But out on the edge—away from the bubble—we are forced to engage with unfiltered ideas and opinions. People on the margins think outside of our church's culture and discipleship systems. Their ideas get us thinking differently about our leadership and our partnerships. It may feel counterintuitive, but God meets us out there on the edge. The margins are where our assumptions are challenged and our conventions reevaluated. On the edge we become pioneers rather than settlers. And when we're looking out, we experience new life.

These three personal postures—looking back, looking up, and looking out—prepare our hearts to reproduce renewal work in others. It positions us to make the kind of bold choices that are necessary to move back from fossilizing to a dynamic and renewed work of God. But if an organization is going to experience renewal, it's not just personal postures that are necessary; bold organizational choices are necessary as well.

The Dynamics of Organizational Renewal

Keeping a network or church from the decline of movement to machine to monument is no simple matter, but I want to suggest two organizational habits that will help us accomplish this goal—(1) multiplication and (2) gritty intentionality:

Let's begin with *multiplication*. If we want organizational renewal, we must become deeply acquainted with the word *multiply*. Simple, I know. Yet it's an essential part of what it means to thrive and flourish as a church or network. Even in a fallen world, healthy organisms multiply. God designed it to be this way from the beginning.

This idea of multiplication is deeply embedded in what it means to experience renewal. It's an essential part of what it means to thrive and flourish as a church or network.

In Genesis 1, God multiplied his image by creating man and woman. Then he commanded our first parents to be fruitful and *multiply* and fill the earth. After the flood, the same command is repeated to Noah. Then in Genesis 12:2–3 (NIV), God tells Abraham, "I will make you into a great nation, . . . and all peoples on earth will be blessed through you." Throughout the Old Testament, God promises again and again to multiply his people.

So it shouldn't surprise us that when we arrive in the New Testament, God calls the Twelve to multiply. Jesus commands multiplication in the Great Commission (Matthew 28:19). Then in Acts, "the word of God increased and multiplied" (12:24), believers multiplied, and churches multiplied. In 2 Timothy 2:2, we are called to multiply ministry to the next generation. It's hard to read our Bibles and miss God's commitment and call to multiplication.

In Romans 15:19, the apostle Paul says something that is nothing short of incredible. He says, "From Jerusalem and all the way around to Illyricum *I have fulfilled the ministry of the gospel of Christ*" (emphasis added). It's as though Paul is looking back at the last stage of his ministry and hanging up a "Mission Accomplished" banner. But how can this be? Is the ministry of the gospel ever done?

Let's take a moment and unpack Paul's astonishing statement. Illyricum was the region above Macedonia that ran parallel to Italy. Paul believed the ministry of the gospel had been fulfilled—the mission was accomplished and the Great Commission satisfied—from Illyricum all the way back to Jerusalem.

What creates this sense of accomplishment? Was it that Paul had preached the gospel to every lost person? I don't think that's it. Was it that Paul had published gospel literature that everybody was reading? Had he mastered a new technology that would get the gospel into every household? While these are all legitimate pursuits that Christians should continue, they aren't what Paul had in mind.

No, Paul's extraordinary statement must be assigned to one reality. Paul had planted local churches from Jerusalem to

Illyricum. For Paul, fulfilling the ministry of the gospel meant *multiplying churches.*

In Douglas Moo's commentary on Romans, he quotes John Knox:

> He could say that he had completed the preaching of the gospel from Jerusalem to Illyricum only because this statement would have meant for him that the message had been proclaimed and the church planted in each of the nations north and west across Asia Minor and the Greek peninsula—"proclaimed" widely enough and "planted" firmly enough to ensure that the name of Christ would soon be heard throughout its borders.[13]

Paul started strong local churches— churches that were in strategic centers. And Paul was confident that people in each region would soon hear the name of Christ *through the evangelistic efforts of the church.* For this reason, he could say that the ministry of the gospel was complete. For the first apostles, church planting was the center point of Great Commission strategy. The same should be true for us.

Right now, pastors and leaders are reading this book and praying, "Lord, help our church and network to be on mission. Help us to put the Great Commission into action." Well, friends, the way we do mission today is the same way it was done in the New Testament: We multiply. We plant local churches.

Churches fuel missions. They fund missions. They are the fruit of missions. They are the *point* of missions. When you open the New Testament to study missions, you're just studying church planting. That's why Paul was sent from churches and why he was received by churches. That's why Paul's labors resulted in churches. It's why his letters were addressed to churches. Networks and churches are at their best when they're looking to replicate and multiply churches!

But it gets even better. Multiplication is both a mission to the world *and* a megavitamin for the church. For a church to be truly healthy, it must exist for something outside of itself. Multiplication catalyzes church renewal. When we neglect it, our churches bend inward and we are unable to see beyond ourselves. But when we pray and plan for multiplication, we enjoy the revitalizing nourishment that can only come from an outward push.

The Sea of Galilee and the Dead Sea are both fed from the same source, but the Sea of Galilee is teeming with life while the Dead Sea, aptly named, is dark and, well, dead. What makes the difference? Outlets. When life flows *into* and *from* the body, it is sustained *within* the body. The same is true for the church. Though fed from a good source, a local church will die without outlets for multiplication.

A Dead Sea culture makes a church sterile—though that church was once itself a plant! It's sad when church planters gladly start their work through the generosity and the sacrifices of others but have no burden to do the same for the next generation once their church grows and is established. Multiplication was the doorway to mission for them, but that door locks behind them.

Absent a commitment to develop and send planters, local churches settle for community, care, and the corporation. What's missing from that list is *mission*, and it's not incidental. Reproduction, after all, is an essential ingredient for life.

It's true for networks too. When partnerships neglect multiplication, growth comes predominantly from the outside. Thank God for churches and planters who want to join our thing. I believe God has these "brothers and sisters from another mother" all over the place for your network. But a more significant sign of organizational health is seen in homegrown leadership—the fruit of our churches multiplying leaders. I mean, if we must pillage other networks to secure our own future, we're being parasites. But if we have the kind of leadership and discipleship that can produce homegrown planters, we're a life-giving organism. We remain a movement.

And that leads us to the second habit for organizational renewal—*gritty intentionality*. For multiplication to happen, we must put our convictions and beliefs about the mission into practice. I believe that the mission of church planting keeps a dynamic of sacrifice alive in the church. It builds life and vitality into our congregations, which is why the Australian church leader David Penman once said—and I love this quote— "No local church can afford to go without the encouragement and nourishment that will come to it by sending away its best people."[14]

Now I know there are church leaders reading this book who have done that. You've sent away your best people, and I hope you feel God's pleasure as you've made sacrifices to see the gospel go forward. But for every ten churches who have sacrificially multiplied, there are literally thousands who lack the vision and pathway to see their church revitalized through "sending away its best people." For them the next step is not the sacrifice of sending but the galvanizing groundwork of intentional discipleship.

In the Great Commission, Jesus makes clear that *multiplication starts with discipleship*. Pop the hood on the Great Commission and you find a command where the controlling verb—"make disciples"—powers the other participles ("go," "baptize," and "teach").[15] It's no exaggeration to say that the engine of the Great Commission is stamped with disciple making.[16] For any network or family of churches, the vital call to multiply disciples becomes the first step in church planting. If we want to experience renewal, if we truly want to multiply, we must start here.

At a minimum, church planting requires identifying leaders within your church body, training them, releasing them to start new works, and then giving them your support. Our churches and our networks—whether large or small—must be committed to this end. We must raise up leaders and send them to plant. As Paul writes in 2 Timothy 2:2, "What you have heard from me in the presence of many witnesses entrust to faithful men, who will be able to teach others also."

I believe that the future of the church rests on healthy pastors and elder teams intentionally pouring into the new generation. It's essential that networks invest their energy and money into this as well. Our initiatives—training programs, resources, assessment processes, and support—must disciple and support the next generation of planters.

And if we're going to disciple the next generation of planters, we must be intentional about discipling the next generation of Christians before they're called to be a part of a plant. Each church in our networks should have a clear discipleship path for its members. Faithfully making disciples is the only way to identify future leaders. But when we're faithfully making disciples, we're creating a conduit for future planters as well.

When our families of churches treasure the gospel so much that multiplication becomes the air we breathe—the ecosystem in which we live—we'll also experience renewal. And when we become intentional about discipleship and renewal, we become people that define success in terms of reproduction—not by how much we grow but by how much life we give.

Staying Awake During the Revolution

Think back to Rip Van Winkle. He partied. He dozed. He slumbered. When he awoke and looked around, history had passed him by. A government had been overturned and a revolution fought and won—all while he slept. It reminds me of the old proverb:

> A little sleep, a little slumber,
>> a little folding of the hands to rest,
> and poverty will come upon you like a robber,
>> and want like an armed man. (Proverbs 24:33–34)

Take a moment to think about your network or church. Look up from this book and consider the culture you treasure in the group you love and lead. What values have shaped your vision and inspired your sacrifice? If you cherish them, don't let organizational inertia impoverish your ministry while you sleep. Your values and vision can be lost in only five years of slumber. Five years.

Leader, the future is beaming with possibilities for the gospel. Don't fall asleep. Don't slumber while the revolution rages. Tend the gospel fire in your soul. Respect the organizational tensions and pursue renewal dynamics. Think personally, then organizationally.

May God help us stay awake during the revolution. Only then will we bring the glory to God that comes from sustainable ministries. Only then will we be able to pass along a living movement to the next generation.

A KINGDOM MINDSET

Against Tribalism

As I write today, I'm sitting in my office. My weekly work-space sits in a church building where I don't pastor—alongside a team that is unaffiliated with the network I lead. Sounds unusual, doesn't it? Do you know what's even more unusual? The elders at Summit Church in Fort Myers, Florida, provide this office space to me rent-free. Why? Because they genuinely love serving another church planting network.

Summit's vision for impacting others through the gospel extends far beyond providing office space to a friend. Each month, Summit designates about 20 percent of their budget for missions. But only a portion of that (3–4 percent of their total budget) is sent to their denomination and church planting network. The overwhelming majority of their missions giving is sent to other ministries outside those partnerships.

In a world where churches and denominational groups suf-fer from a *scarcity mentality*—which bends them away from generosity toward transactional giving—Summit gives abun-dantly to groups that may never reciprocate. They're committed to spreading the glorious news of the Savior all over the world, even if groups to which they give are never able to return their kindness.

What breaks a church or network free from the gravitational pull of their own interests? What moves a group of leaders to affiliate wholeheartedly while giving globally? What ultimately convinces an elder team that God's mission is bigger than their tribe?

It's the *kingdom of God*.

Thy Kingdom Come

From the time of the Old Testament judges until the rule of Israel's three great kings—Saul, David, and Solomon—the Israelites lived primarily under foreign domination. Then after Solomon's reign, a civil war ensued between Israel's northern tribes and Judah. Against the backdrop of national disobedience, betrayal, war, and exile, God delivered a promise to the nation: the Day of the Lord would come when the Messiah would unite Israel and establish his kingdom.

Then God became man, and the kingdom Christ inaugurated was wholly outside conventional expectations. Before Christ, many Jews believed the kingdom would be established through military might. But instead of a glorious and visible dominion, Jesus brought a bewildering announcement: "The kingdom of God is at hand; repent and believe in the gospel" (Mark 1:15). What could this mean? If repentance was necessary to enter the kingdom, surely the people who needed to repent were the Roman invaders.

Instead, Jesus confronted *every* human being. He announced a kingdom that invades our broken world like a mustard seed—unassuming, unanticipated, and mysterious, sown quietly but expanding unpredictably (Mark 4:30–34).

Can you see what the Savior announced? Jesus' kingdom is a patient yet potent occupation, a counterinsurgency poised to surreptitiously bear fruit across the globe. Every Christmas is a reminder that when Jesus arrived, the kingdom dawned and the powers of darkness began to lose their grip on the world (Matthew 12:28). The King came to claim his throne and welcome his people into the blessings of his divine reign. His kingdom is *already* present, and yet its full consummation has *not yet* come.

When we adopted our son Asa, there was a nine-month waiting period between the *termination* of the birthparents' rights and the *finalization* of the adoption. During that tenuous time, it *felt* like Asa was our son. After all, he lived with us, we loved him, and we were parenting him. But the new family symbolized by his placement was not yet a legal reality. He was *already* in the home, but *not yet* adopted.

> *Every Christmas is a reminder that when Jesus arrived, the kingdom dawned and the powers of darkness began to lose their grip on the world.*

Already, but not yet. This idea, coined by theologian Geerhardus Vos in the early twentieth century, describes the tensions between what we already experience of the kingdom in this life and the benefits that still await us. We are already saved (Ephesians 2:8), but not fully (Romans 5:9). We already know Jesus Christ (2 Corinthians 4:6), but not in the way we will know him (1 Corinthians 13:12). We are already adopted (Romans 8:15), but await final adoption (Romans 8:23). We have already been judged (John 5:24), but the final judgment seat will come (2 Corinthians 5:10).

The gospel—the good news embodied in the birth, life, death, and resurrection of Jesus—*already* fulfills the Old Testament's kingdom hopes and expectations. But the consummation has *not yet* come. Christ came as the true Adam (Luke 3:23–38; Romans 5:18–21; 1 Corinthians 15:20–22), the seed of Abraham (Galatians 3:16), the true Israel (Matthew 2:15; Luke 4:1–13), and the Son of David (2 Samuel 23:3; Matthew 1:6; 17) to announce the kingdom's arrival, but not its completion (Matthew 1:15).

We inhabit what Oscar Cullman called "the dialectic of present and future" where the future and present ages have overlapped.[1] "The church lives 'between the times,'" wrote George Eldon Ladd. "The old age goes on, but the powers of the new age have irrupted [*forcibly entered*] into the old age."[2]

A Kingdom Vision

The point of this kingdom talk is not to press my eschatology or even to influence you toward a particular hermeneutic. I've shared my take on the kingdom, and you may nuance it differently. Regardless, when we see the kingdom's arrival in Christ, it inevitably lifts our eyes above our churches and tribes to God's larger work in the world. When we think about God's activity on earth, "the kingdom" gets us looking through telescopes rather than microscopes.

Do you remember microscope days in science class? In my class, we were liberated from our desks and free to roam about the classroom. Even better, sometimes Mr. Rowell tossed in an amphibian dissection and issued every kid a scalpel. I miss the days when public schools mandated frog surgery and armed ninth graders with lethal weapons.

Looking into a microscope draws our gaze downward and concentrates our focus. Telescopes work differently. They draw our vision up and out. They take big, faraway objects and bring them close. Microscopes make small things big; telescopes make big things near and clear.

With a kingdom mindset, we focus our vision on God's big

and beautiful work outside our smaller fields of vision. We live in a small corner of the church. But a kingdom mindset brings the larger picture closer to our heart. It girds us with three big reminders:

Reminder #1: Our churches are not the kingdom. The kingdom is God's dynamic rule and reign unleashed in his creation. It's more than where his subjects gather. When people enter God's kingdom, they come under his loving reign, and they keep the King of love himself at the center of their worship. Ultimately, then, the church derives its existence from the kingdom. It doesn't work the other way around.

With a kingdom mindset, we focus our vision on God's big and beautiful work outside our smaller fields of vision.

When the church is confused with the kingdom, we are in danger of moving away from the way of love and manipulating the levers of power.

Sometimes this approach has happened *corporately.* Christians throughout history have unleashed untold injustices due to their belief that God authorized them to subordinate pagan peoples to the church's rule. The atrocities born of this failure call us to both blush and grieve.

Other times it happens *individually.* Leaders can be tempted to relocate God's authority from the Bible to their office in the church. This bad theology leads to authoritarian practice, celebrity leaders, cultures of groupthink, and tribalism.

A wise leader understands that the kingdom and the church are distinct. This truth protects us from dangers and brings benefits.

When the GCC team and board defined the values that would guide our work, *kingdom focus* became a way to describe one of our deep burdens. We define kingdom focus as a commitment to "actively serve, learn from, and partner with ministries outside GCC." This value captured convictions that are core to our institutional identity:

- *We believe our collective should not be self-contained.* Important things that we must learn come to us from outside our group.
- *We recognize God is at work in powerful ways outside our tribe.* A kingdom focus helps us diligently look for the places where God is working in others and then celebrate what we see.
- *We recognize the temptation to reduce God's activity to what he is doing in us.* We drift toward seeing our collective at the apex of God's activity. We need to pray, "Your kingdom come, your will be done, on earth as it is in heaven" (Matthew 6:10). Recognizing these desires and temptations guards our network against pridefully conflating God's larger work with what he's doing in us.

Reminder #2: The church witnesses to the kingdom. The church does not build or become the kingdom; it exists to testify to the King's glory and love. We follow the One who "went throughout all the cities and villages, teaching in their synagogues and proclaiming the gospel of the kingdom and healing every disease and every affliction" (Matthew 9:35).

The church belongs to two ages—the one we occupy and the one yet to come. While here, we are called to make the invisible kingdom visible through our words and works.

The church belongs to two ages—the one we occupy and the one yet to come. While here, we are called to make the invisible kingdom visible through our words and works. We proclaim the King's good news, and we validate the reality and potency of the kingdom in our love for one another and our neighbor.

Reminder #3: The kingdom offers a permanent affiliation.
Families fray, ministries end, and churches once formative to
many no longer exist. Jesus announced that even marriage—
often seen as the locus of self-fulfillment—exists only in this
world (Matthew 22:30). Where does one find membership
that lasts?

Our most durable identity is our kingdom citizenship
that unites us permanently with believers around the globe.
Remembering this truth tamps down our tendency to think first
about our national heritage, political party, or sports fandom.

R. C. Sproul was once invited to Eastern Europe for a series
of teaching engagements. His tour ended in Romania, but his
team was warned that the Romanian border guards were hostile
to Americans. Sure enough, when the train reached Romania,
two burly guards climbed aboard.

The two men spoke broken English, and they were brusque
and rude. They gestured for passports, and when one guard
noticed a woman in the group holding a paper bag in her lap,
he said, "What this? What in bag?" The officer snatched the
bag and pulled out a Bible. And Sproul thought, *Uh-oh, now
we're in trouble.*

But then as the officer leafed through the Bible's pages, he
stopped and looked at Dr. Sproul. Holding Sproul's American
passport, he said, "You no American." Then he looked at the
woman and said, "You no American." Then, surprisingly, he
said, "I am not Romanian. Read what it says." The preacher
looked down at the man's finger pointing to Philippians 3:20:
"Our citizenship is in heaven."

The officer was a Christian! With a big smile he turned to
his subordinates and said, "Let these people alone. They're OK.
They're Christians."[3]

Every leader should love their tribe. But the doctrine of

God's kingdom reminds us that our tribes are temporal while the kingdom is eternal. The prudent leader builds temporal alliances and keeps earthly commitments in love while making eternal affiliation his chief anchor.

The Kingdom and the Tribe

That brings us to the importance of the kingdom for our partnerships. Churches, networks, and denominations enjoy connection on two different levels—the kingdom level and the tribal level. The kingdom is our gospel priority, but our tribe rightly takes a functional priority.

Kingdom Connection, a Gospel Priority

Admission to the kingdom springs from *the new birth*—each believer's conversion and baptism. As Jesus said, "Truly, truly, I say to you, unless one is born again he cannot see the kingdom of God" (John 3:3). As a result, kingdom citizenship is a privilege of the gospel, and making disciples who become "fellow citizens with the saints" (Ephesians 2:19) is a gospel priority.

Our kingdom citizenship shouldn't discourage our closer alliances to networks and denominations (see below). Functionally speaking, kingdom collaboration is secondary to our tribal commitments. But kingdom connections are still highly strategic. Our kingdom theology reminds us that the more we move toward exclusivity, separatism, or making our tribe the only tribe, the more we move away from experiencing the beauty and scope of our crucified King's rule.

The scope of the kingdom is *global*. When we submit to Jesus as our king, we become subjects in his worldwide kingdom. Christians all over the globe share a common king, a mutual law, a joint allegiance, a united mission, and the same eternal destination. For this reason, it's a good thing for local churches to enter broad partnerships with other gospel-preaching churches that differ on secondary matters.

We have a New Testament impulse for this kind of ministry that harnesses diverse churches for the sake of greater kingdom impact. Mission agencies that help gospel-believing churches lock arms to get the message of Christ to the unreached are essential. Agencies that help diverse churches—even ones that don't have the same doctrinal understanding of baptism or the Lord's Supper—work together to serve people impacted by a hurricane or tornado are essential as well. After all, Christ's love demands I help you when you're hurting, even if I don't agree with you theologically (Luke 10:25–37).

Citizenship in the kingdom connects us to the *local and global work of God*. As kingdom citizens, we pray for its advance: "Our Father in heaven, . . . your kingdom come, your will be done, on earth as it is in heaven" (Matthew 6:9–10).

But a kingdom mindset also pulls us beyond the confines of our own backyard toward *kingdom collaboration*—loving, listening, learning, and at times laboring with citizens who share our kingdom but live outside of our castle. In our kingdom role, we don't serve in order to curry favor or build an empire, but rather to invest in what God is doing in our community and to the outermost parts of the world.

Tribal Collaboration, Our Functional Priority

Admission to the tribe. When I use the term *tribe*, I'm describing the more intimate connection between churches in the same network or denomination. Your tribe is your principal extra-local partnership, the denominational entity or network group to which your church has made a commitment.

The scope of our tribes. Churches enter tribes by choice as a direct result of their alignment with the doctrine, vision, and values of the group. The tribe is limited to the circle of churches and leaders who are committed to it.

In the early church, partnerships between churches produced an ecosystem from which mission and care flowed. But for any ecosystem to thrive, there must be tensions and balances. Different species must learn to cohabitate harmoniously with other species, without giving up what makes them distinct or what they need in order to survive.

Our role in the tribe. The good of one's tribe must be situated within the greatness of God's kingdom, but we must also see that the kingdom connection works best when our local tribal relationships remain our functional priority.

At the beginning of this chapter, I described Summit Church's kingdom generosity. But if for some reason Summit had to cut its missions budget severely, it probably would not begin by cutting its giving to partners with whom they are most closely affiliated. Every organization with finite capacities must prioritize their relationships. Recognizing differences in time and energy allocation between a close tribal commitment and a broader kingdom commitment is right and good.

Beware the Vice: Tribalism

But there's a danger. Absent the virtue of a kingdom mindset, churches, networks, and denominations develop partnership scoliosis—an inward curvature away from God's larger kingdom purposes toward their own tribal affiliations.

It's *tribalism*, a malady that ultimately starves the God-installed drive for greater kingdom good. Tribalism is a closing loop, a dangerous virus left untreated by the vitamins of a kingdom vision. And when the tribalism virus grows, autonomy absolutizes, the collective corrupts, and the stock on personhood plummets.

It may seem surprising, but when tribal autonomy is idolized, people—even the people in our tribe—are less valued, not more. When we're bent inward and can't see beyond our own borders, our group infatuation dulls our drive to learn from those outside of our stream. The gene pool by which we measure effectiveness and honestly evaluate ourselves narrows. The celebration of *our* ministry and *our* leaders becomes the driving ethos. Then, sadly, the network culture grows loveless and utilitarian—a spiritualized version of *Lord of the Flies*.

> *When the tribalism virus grows, autonomy absolutizes, the collective corrupts, and the stock on personhood plummets.*

Network leaders and pastors must resist this enticement. There must be a clear-sighted acknowledgment of the dangers of a tribe-only mindset. After all, tribalism has a way of accentuating and catalyzing many of the other vices I've written about in this book. It leads directly to the dangers of egotism and triumphalism, which we'll explore in the final two chapters.

When leaders build a kingdom-less culture, tribalism emerges. Networks become fiefdoms that serve at the pleasure of leaders' platforms. Self-obsessed people demand loyalty rather than winning it, and their teams—when they have them—demonstrate a predictable partisanship for the leader's way.

Under tribalism's influence, everything must be done "the network way," and fruitful unity in diversity is destroyed. Service feels forced, not voluntary. There's no genuine partnership based on conviction and collaborative vision. Gone is the sense of solidarity that binds people despite their different backgrounds.

When tribalism thrives, a generous culture dies. The tribe-only mentality of hyperindividualist leaders pushes the tribes they lead away from communion and toward consumerism. And when such leaders think about resources, the discussion moves to *me* and *mine*.

Vice Audit 5: Tribalism

Rank the degree to which you agree with the following statements on a scale of 1–5 (5 = strongly agree, 4 = agree, 3 = neutral, 2 = disagree, 1 = strongly disagree). Write your ranking in the blank to the left of each statement.

_____ 1. The celebration of *our* ministry and *our* leaders is our driving ethos.

_____ 2. In our churches, everything must be done "the network way."

_____ 3. It's rare for our church or leadership team to publicly celebrate something God is doing in a church outside of our tribe.

_____ 4. Often our affiliation with our network and denominational group gets top billing, even over our kingdom citizenship.

_____ 5. Our church does not give money except to entities affiliated with our denomination and network.

_____ **Total**

If your church and leadership scored between 0–8, you likely have the kind of culture that embodies a kingdom mindset. If you scored between 9–18, take some time to

---

sit with your leadership team and talk through the three kingdom reminders in the chapter. If you scored between 19–25, your church is in danger of succumbing to tribalism. Take some time to confess this to the Lord and pray that he will help you develop a love for his larger kingdom work.

A few years back, a group known as the Bolton Forgers produced a preponderance of fake sculptures and phony paintings. This group united for a single purpose—to con the art world out of serious money. According to Scotland Yard, the ring made millions on their scams.

At its worst, tribalism makes Christian leaders like those forgers, uniting gifted teams merely for the sake of personal gain and selfish legacy. The trouble is that the act of forging misapplies our gifts. When the police eventually raided the Boltons' property, the work and tools they found there—including a furnace for melting silver and a random bust of Thomas Jefferson tossed into the corner—became the evidence used to indict them.

When we team up to use our God-given gifts for self, we miss eternal opportunities. We sacrifice the glory of interdependence, Christlike humility, and the yearning to live in service of something larger than ourselves. Gospel-conceived and grace-infused kingdom motivations lie dormant within tribalized leaders—if they live at all.

If you see yourself or your group in any of these descriptions, consider this question: How does the good news of God's kingdom help you in your struggles against tribalism? What steps can you take to fight against a tribe-only mindset and move toward fruitful and lasting connections.

The Way of the Kingdom Is Love

The answer to these questions—the heart of a kingdom mind-set—is love. As the Beatles sang, "Love is all you need"—um . . . *God's love*, that is. Love is the kingdom way because it displays the King's heart. As Dane Ortlund writes,

> God's love is as boundless as God himself. This is why the apostle Paul speaks of divine love as a reality that stretches to an immeasurable "breadth and length and height and depth" (Eph. 3:18)—the only thing in the universe as immeasurable as that is God himself. God's love is as expansive as God himself.
>
> For God to cease to love his own, God would need to cease to exist, because God does not simply have love; he is love (1 John 4:16).[4]

But God's love is not formless and abstract. His eternal character is expressed in the promises he makes and the death he suffered on our behalf. In the Bible, God's loving promises surface in covenants—God's public vows to his people. Christian weddings, wherein the love of a man and woman are expressed in the exchange of public vows, reflect this same reality. It's a timeless truth: *biblical love expresses itself in commitment*. And as the heart motivation that fuels God's essence, the fire of God's love in Christ burns away self-interest, refining our tribal commitments and purifying our passion for broader kingdom impact.

How Does God's Love Fuel Tribal Commitments?

First, God's love invites church leaders to make and keep commitments. When you think about it, partnerships are built on a foundation of faith in God's ordained model for ministry, and they grow as the parties involved make mutual, familial affirmations to one another. Like the most important economies in the Christian faith—marriage, family, salvation, and the church—partnerships are built on the concept (if not the reality) of a covenant.[5] Paul E. Miller explains *hesed*, the biblical concept of "covenant love," this way:

> Sometimes *hesed* is translated "steadfast love." It combines commitment with sacrifice. *Hesed* is one-way love. Love without an exit strategy. When you love with *hesed* love, you bind yourself to the object of your love, no matter what the response is. So if the object of your love snaps at you, you still love that person. If you've had an argument with your spouse in which you were slighted or not heard, you refuse to retaliate through silence or withholding your affection. Your response to the other person is entirely independent of how that person has treated you. *Hesed* is a stubborn love.[6]

To cut a covenant is simply to make and keep promises. And those promises define the contours of the commitment by outlining appropriate mutual expectations. I'm not unpacking covenant language because I think network connections must include signing a covenant. But a covenant mindset of love and commitment lays the foundation on which every partnership is built. A commitment does not carry the same weight as a formal covenant. Commitments include both rights and obligations, but the real glue for a commitment is not the rights it engenders but the love it calls forth.

God is most glorified when committed tribes throw themselves wholeheartedly toward one another in fulfillment of their promises. Biblical love, after all, does not keep accounts or measure who is most invested during each stage of the relationship. Rather, it keeps *sacrifice* at the center. Commitments exist to reflect the promise-keeping nature of God.

God is most glorified when committed tribes throw themselves wholeheartedly toward one another in fulfillment of their promises.

Networks will thrive only if we cultivate the character necessary for unity—mercy, the practice of forgiveness, friendship across differences, honesty, and love. It's not our systems and strategies that will keep us together. It's not even doctrine (unless that doctrine moves you toward love). It's our commitment to invest in relationships and the Spirit's power to help us stick it out. Without this commitment, our movements will become monuments within one generation.

Second, loving commitments become a means to strengthening local churches. The true measure of a mature leader can be seen in the commitments they make and how diligently these commitments are fulfilled. Leadership can be treacherous terrain, but for most leaders, an average week will include being encouraged, preferred, and affirmed in their gifts. Often leaders are the objects of loyal commitments.

Church planting networks are places where pastors are encouraged to move in the opposite direction. They are the ones who *make* loving commitments. Yes, it will work against that part of their mind that screams, *If I add one more thing, I will implode!* But the commitments a network asks for are designed to prevent the implosion, not speed it along.

A local pastor's character is built through habitual acts of loving service—certainly this is true within the church, but it's also true when the pastor's service is given to outside leaders who won't readily defer to them. As leaders, we need to serve others who aren't overly impressed with our church's budget or size. In the rhythms, rituals, and relationships found in a church planting network, pastors can find themselves recipients of other leaders' gifts, perspectives, and kindnesses. In these open and dependent relationships, pastors learn just how much we need others.

I believe network commitments should be specific and defined. Many church leaders affirm both a specific commitment to their local church and insist that their church joins with a larger organization—whether a denomination or network—that will help their church become the best it can be. Why is this the case? Just as a defined commitment to a local church gives us personal opportunities to apply our love for Christ through specific actions, a defined network commitment helps churches live out a dependent and other-centered life organizationally.

Finally, loving tribal commitments provide an ecosystem for growth and flourishing. A collective is not merely a *collection* of autonomous churches or denominationally bound leaders. More importantly, it's a group of *connected* pastors and churches, growing and flourishing together because they're helping each other.

Eugene Peterson once planted a church in Bel Air, Maryland, and he received funding from his Presbyterian denomination. As part of the funding arrangement, Peterson had to complete a multipage "new church development" form each month that reported numerical statistics and provided a space to summarize the state of his ministry and soul.

Over time, Peterson became convinced that the denomination did not read the reports. In fact, he figured they never flipped beyond the first page, which meant the handwritten section about his soul and ministry went unread.

To test this theory, Peterson concocted fictional stories

that portrayed his slow ministerial disintegration. He began with a tale of growing depression that rendered him unable to sleep, pray, or perform his pastoral duties. When he heard nothing, he upped the ante and created a drinking problem, which eventually led him to craft a story of preaching while sloppy drunk. In the report, Peterson would ask questions like, "I think I need treatment. How should I go about getting it? Are there funds available?"

He heard nothing, so he became bolder.

Peterson invented a fictious affair replete with torrid love-making in the sanctuary. He was, of course, discovered by a church member. But not to worry. Peterson then discovered that the church was full of swingers. The Sunday after his adultery was discovered, attendance doubled.

Months passed. Peterson created even more outrageous fiction. Liturgies including psychedelic mushrooms? Why not! Each month the reports became more excruciatingly exaggerated.

When his three years of support from the church development fund was complete, Peterson debriefed with the committee. He asked why he couldn't get help with his depression, sexual addiction, and abuse of hallucinogens in the Eucharist. The committee was dumbfounded, so Peterson told them the story.

They were not amused.

Peterson's story incites more sadness than humor. Yes, he was connected to a group of churches. But he was entirely alone. No one seemed to care. Peterson recalled, "The people who ordained me and took responsibility for my work were interested in financial reports, attendance graphs, program planning. But they were not interested in *me*. They were interested in my job; they cared little for my vocation."[7]

In a healthy network, the good we give should flow up and down the organizational chart. In the best networks, commitment is collaborative. You can share with anyone about any given subject on any given day.

How Does Love Push Us beyond Our Tribe?

While order and leadership must be present, healthy networks must not display the self-interested hierarchies of tribalism. Instead, we are to be willing to look outside our tribe and even ask uncomfortable questions such as, "How do we become a family of churches where people who are different—perhaps those who represent ethnic minorities—feel more welcome? How do we become a network where we can experience diversity without a blindness to the reality that our language and social norms are not always normative for other cultures? Diverse friends enrich thinking," observes Isaac Adams, "and we're simply going to have to have more speeds than 'heretic' and 'faithful' if we're going to speak with each other."[8]

When networks are willing to ask such questions, we'll start to see beyond our own skin and experience the kind of redemptive kingdom diversity we will encounter in heaven when the kingdom is consummated (Revelation 7:9). Not because it's fashionable, chic, or politically correct—but because our experience of the gospel forms us into a dynamic movement that achieves together what no church can accomplish alone.

Our tribe should be a place that makes us better, not a place for consumers or those who crave distinction or unity without diversity. Such motivation tears at the social fabric that binds us together. Instead, our networks ought to

Our tribe should be a place that makes us better, not a place for consumers or those who crave distinction or unity without diversity.

have cultures that call us to a manner of life worthy of the gospel (Philippians 1:27).

The Big Kingdom Picture

Think back over your life. Most of us treasure memories of things we've accomplished with other leaders who inexplicably improved us. Maybe it was your picking up new insights, planting churches, addressing stubborn needs, or worshiping with other leaders at a conference or event. These are the flashes where our birth and life make the most sense, the times when our calling crystalizes with meaning. They are the Eric Liddell "when I run, I feel his pleasure" moments. They are the moments when we feel most alive—when the marriage of our gifts and our call is united with others in the pursuit of a glorious cause.

In those moments, the huge *I* behind tribalism bows to the *we* of your elders, your tribe, or the kingdom. And when your mind is left to drift back to those days, you know that the experience of flourishing was part of why you were created. That what you accomplished together was so much more important—more intrinsically valuable—than you could have ever accomplished on your own.

The biblical ideal—expressed in both tribal and larger kingdom partnerships—is something worthy of your life. Yes, it will cost you. More than you know! A hobbling limp awaits those who will give their lives for the sake of others. But the true heroes are not those who behold the mission's magnificence and then return to their chateau. True heroes are the ones who train, serve, sleep, and bleed on the mountain of mission until their sacrifices finally enable those they lead to ascend the peak.

Deep in the recesses of our soul we know this to be true.

With our eyes held close to the kingdom telescope and examples like Summit Church before us, we commit to this together. And God promises us courage to preach boldly, witness wisely, suffer resiliently, send frequently, and believe the gospel unshakably. As we stand firm in our commitment to God and our affection for one another, we model for the world how being a servant in God's kingdom inspires our dreams and makes life worth living.

PART

THE CHARACTER
OF PARTNERSHIP

HUMILITY

Against Egotism

Ten years ago, I found myself in an unexpected season when the scope of my ministry role was reduced. For many years I had been near the center of a growing movement that was planting churches and training leaders. It was exhilarating. But things happened in a way I could not have predicted, which made it impossible for me to remain in that role. After close to three decades in the same church and network, we hit the reset button. Life started over.

Whether God was humbling or rescuing me, I honestly do not know. Surprising doors of opportunity flew open, but the whole situation still felt like a precipitous fall from grace. I found myself downshifting from a network-wide leadership role to sitting quietly in elders' meetings, racing to learn an entirely new church culture.

To compound matters, the group I left tended to interpret departures as disloyalty. Relational doors slammed shut. Much of what I had spent my adult life building seemed to be erased—or at least sealed off—as though it no longer mattered. It wasn't just the relational reshuffling, but my disappointed dreams opened wounds as well. *How did I get here?* I lamented,

What in the world is God doing? To be brutally honest, it felt like God had defrauded me.

There was no dramatic event or angelic encounter. But as one month swallowed another, my sense of displacement, sprinkled with grains of desperation, ignited a hunger to adapt and learn in exile. In my old world, I had the credibility of a tenured expert. To move forward into my new world, I had to think like a pupil. As a result, my expectations had to be put on a diet until a smaller role began to fit.

Over time, God cultivated my palette to fit my place. My craving to know God's purpose shifted toward a thirst to trust his providence. Eventually, the pangs diminished. Confidence in God's sovereignty satisfied my soul, and I began to view the table of ministry with a different appetite.

Ultimately, I landed back in the world of leading a growing church planting network. But it would have never occurred without the soul-shaping, innovation-sparking, vision-clearing shift that accompanied a lower place and a smaller space.

Networks open the door to a vast frontier of gospel opportunity. In a partnership, leaders find support, a place to identify, and catalytic power to mobilize a community of churches for mission and impact. But too often, networks also become a place where pride finds a platform. We've all seen it. Personality moves to the center. Power is consolidated. Popularity is prioritized. Collaboration deteriorates to a principle with no practice, and an ecosystem is formed that incubates and then accommodates, falling victim to the vice of *egotism.*

> **Too often, networks become places where pride finds a platform.**

I like to think networks exist so celebrities will not. But to avoid this vice of egotism, we must understand what makes it attractive. And then, together, we must flee to the One who embodies the vice-crushing virtue of *humility.*

Beware the Vice: Egotism

Few things compromise the success of a network more than leaders who seek to use the collective as a platform for their own glory. In chapter 3, I wrote about the vice of radical individualism. Egotism and celebrity ambitions are what happen when radical individualism finds a microphone and a podcast.

For the egotistical leader, the network experience is measured by whether their agenda is satisfied, their name is growing, their church is perceived as more influential, their turf is protected, and their gifts are being recognized and celebrated. Something very good—their ambition for glory—has been corrupted by the object on which it is fixed. *Themselves.*

Just to be clear: Loving glory or desiring to use your gifts to serve God is not bad. Each of us is born with an instinct for glory. It comes factory installed within every human person. Glory arrests our attention. It grabs us. It arouses something in our souls. Our hard wiring for glory is why we are awed by great comebacks, heroic efforts, sacrificial endurance, and extraordinary talents. A favorite team clinches a playoff spot, or we read about astonishing perseverance in the face of opposition—like William Wilberforce prevailing over the British Parliament to end the slave trade. Such glories call us to do something that matters, to use our gifts for a greater good, to unite to seek an ambition greater than our own puny existence.

Paul's letter to the Romans portrays two groups of seekers who embody our glory impulse. On one side are "those who by patience in well-doing *seek for glory* and honor and immortality"; on the other side are "those who are *self-seeking.*" To the first group,

God doesn't oppose glory seeking; he commends it. And what's more astounding is he rewards it with eternal life.

God "will give eternal life"; for the second, "there will be wrath and fury" (Romans 2:7–8, emphasis added). Pause to ponder this: God doesn't oppose glory seeking; he *commends* it. And what's more astounding is he rewards it with eternal life.

When our glory drive is turned toward God, it's called ambition—a wondrous, God-installed thing to behold. But when the hardwired desire for glory is infected with self, noble ambitions collapse (Philippians 2:3; James 3:14) The quest for self-glory rules the day, and the leader moves to the center of attention.

If you've kept up with the onslaught of failed church and network leaders, you are undoubtedly familiar with the egotistical cult of celebrity (and the spectacular falls that often accompany it). But I want to be clear. The egotism problem is not identical to popularity or mass appeal. If that were the case, then Jesus himself could have been censured for having a public ministry, one that included adoring fans who waved palm leaves and laid their cloaks at his feet.

I'm convinced there's a vast gray area between being a popular pastor and an egotistical celebrity seeker. Within church and network leadership, there's a spectrum of people with a colorful assortment of mixed motives (Jeremiah 17:9–10). Personally, I hope folks in our collective's churches listen to certain popular pastors. Many of them are popular because they're wise and helpful.

> *Egotistical leaders often build self-centered platforms, ones that later collapse under the weight of their own selfish ambition.*

When I talk about the vice of egotism, I'm thinking instead about *a hunger to seek fame.* For a godly leader, fame can be an understandable (even if undesirable) effect of faithfulness. But egotistical leaders often build self-centered platforms, ones that later collapse under the weight of their own selfish ambition.

If you're tempted to think I have a particular leader in my crosshairs with my observations about the cult of celebrity, let me be quick to say that *I most certainly do.* It's me! Now in my case, becoming an actual celebrity pastor would require that I gain several gifts I do not presently possess—a humongous church, a reliable memory, and a good set of white teeth, to name a few. But my point is that I need look no further than the mirror to see a dangerously egotistical celebrity wannabe.

So in the remainder of this chapter, I want to move away from scrutinizing the big personalities and the most scandalous falls from grace to the task of *self-examination.* Let's look at me and you to see what's at the heart of our own temptation toward egotism:

First, an ego demands distinction. Gifts and abilities bring distinction. Albert Einstein's brilliance earned him an invitation to be the second president of Israel. He declined, but it illustrates the point from Proverbs: "A man's gift makes room for him and brings him before the great" (18:16).

Cultivating a reputation for quality or integrity can also bring distinction. An honest family or business is respected within a community: "A good name is to be chosen rather than great riches" (Proverbs 22:1). We are created in such a way that our flourishing is connected to our sense of influence. Think about our experience with encouragement, which is meaningful because an affirmation helps us see how our life is making a difference.

Moreover, it's normal for a leader to desire distinction. Human beings are not content to simply exist; we long to bring value to others. "Whether they be old or young, rich or poor, high or low, wise or foolish, ignorant or learned," observed John Adams, "every individual is seen to be strongly actuated by a desire to be seen, heard, talked of, approved and respected."[1] That's not any different from being drawn or feeling set apart to lead. The desire for distinction is simply a person saying, "I'm an individual, created and called by God to go and bear fruit" (John 15:16). The desire for distinction arms leaders with a sense of destiny and purpose. So far, so good.

But distinction spoils the soul when it becomes our singular passion, when it moves from being an honor bestowed by others and becomes a right we demand. Have you considered what happens in the soul of a church or church planting network when a good name or reputation becomes an object of worship?

Distinction spoils the soul when it becomes our singular passion, when it moves from being an honor bestowed by others and becomes a right we demand.

Then distinction is no longer a fruit of faithfulness; it instead reshapes the contours of how we define ministry success and becomes a matter of necessity. Timothy Dwight, grandson of Jonathan Edwards, saw this issue as one of the greatest threats to ministry. In the spring of 1814, he addressed the Yale graduating class, warning these future church leaders and church planters about "the love of distinction":

> I will now suppose you to go out into the world under the full influence of the love of distinction, and with a fixed determination to pursue it as the commanding object of your life . . .
>
> Let me exhort you to remember, also, that this spirit will regularly and intensely debase your character . . . Selfishness is in its nature little and base. But no passion and no pursuits are more absolutely selfish than the love of distinction. One's self is here the sole object; and in this object all the labours, pursuits, and wishes terminate.[2]

Dwight delivered this message to ministerial students because church ministry—and the work of church multiplication in particular—makes us more prone to elevate distinction and make it an idol. Think about it. We deal with eternal realities, sharing truths that are timeless for God's church. We prevail against the very powers of hell! As ministers, we've identified with an embattled people who have persevered for two millennia. We're not delusional when we nurture high hopes for the church's perseverance and continuity—there's justifiable evidence!

But the danger of a love of distinction dwells in its subtlety. It masquerades under the guise of seemingly legitimate goals such as ministry influence, gospel expansion, and resource stewardship. Guarding the gospel becomes conflated with protecting the brand. Distinction is no longer the means; it becomes the mission.

The sad truth is that some people will do almost anything to read their name in print. When John Wilkes Booth—the actor who assassinated President Abraham Lincoln at Ford's Theatre—planned the murder, he forgot to prepare for life as a fugitive. Cowering with his broken leg in the Maryland pine thicket, Booth had no shelter and little food. He shivered into a sleepless destitution. Yet his love for inhabiting the center stage would not die. Historian James Swanson describes it this way: "Booth's curiosity about the country's reaction was insatiable, and he beseeched Jones [a nearby officer] to bring all the papers he could. Jones remembered the scene vividly: 'He never tired of the newspapers.'"[3]

Craving distinction makes us love the newspapers. We pour over print in search of praise. Booth was on a quest to be newsworthy at any cost, even if it meant assassinating the president.

Second, an ego avoids honest criticism. Apple employees coined the term "reality distortion field" to describe Steve Jobs's ability to twist any fact to fit his own purpose. "At the root of the reality distortion," wrote biographer Walter Isaacson, "was Jobs's belief that the rules didn't apply to him. He had some evidence for this; in his childhood, he had often been able to bend reality to his desires. Rebelliousness and willfulness were ingrained in his character. He had the sense that he was special, a chosen one, an enlightened one."[4]

Not to throw shade on Steve Jobs, but the world pretty much agrees with his self-assessment. In the world of technology, Jobs *was* special and enlightened. But his self-appraisal made it difficult for him to value and receive criticism from others. After all, when you're the reality-bending superstar on the field, it's hard to see your need for the rest of the team.

But it's dangerous when a leader begins to believe he's above the rules. In the best churches, ministries, and networks, strong leaders are surrounded by other strong leaders—encircled by a cadre of courageous individuals who are willing to name the BS when they smell something funny.

Egotistical pastors often have relational networks or small groups that create the illusion of honesty with little actual accountability. They group with an entourage of friends or family who are enamored with the pastor's gifts, fruit, or leadership instincts. I've written elsewhere that "an enamored entourage too easily becomes a group of enablers, a team whose mode of operation is simply to cut the leader some slack."[5] If a team member's own ego is stroked by accommodating the ego of the lead pastor, the team member becomes a great encourager but a poor corrector, particularly when their salary depends more on their encouragement than their honesty.

Good leaders recognize this, but egotistical leaders don't

typically want to hear about weaknesses. They want loyalty. To a leader swollen with self, hard questions feel like a personal attack. And the sad soul bold enough to pose those questions quickly gets benched. Unless there are two or more people to whom each leader can point and say, "They will be honest even if it hurts me," that leader is probably enjoying *un*-accountability. That person is sliding on slick ice toward egotism.

In Geneva, John Calvin had a network of pastors with whom he shared life. And Calvin had more mental wattage than most folks—like a theological Steve Jobs for the 1500s. But he did not allow his many gifts to insulate him from accountability. "Calvin was but one member of a *company* of pastors and he was willing to submit to its authority and judgment. Calvin's Company of Pastors was never Calvin's per se."[6]

Beware if you find yourself increasingly preoccupied with your persona and less occupied with the mission. It's dangerous when the messenger becomes more important than the message and ministry; it must not be this way in our networks. We all need faithful brothers and sisters willing to risk a wound (Proverbs 27:6), and we need a biblical vision of loyalty that is not defined by personal indebtedness but by fidelity to the Savior.

Third, an ego "uses" institutions. Many leaders don't understand the institutional genetics by which collectives operate. Networks are built on the concept of exchange. When we become a collective of churches, we agree to surrender a sliver of autonomy in exchange for a greater good, such as church planting or leadership formation. As with most institutions, there are trade-offs. We give up some individuality and are molded for the good of the whole. The man who joins the military, for instance, soon discovers he must surrender some of his individuality to find a place within his branch. Be it baseball, Boy Scouts, or the British crown, institutions invite us to trade the supremacy of individuality for the benefits of collective good.

But an egotistical mentality refuses to abandon the priority of self. For the celebrity-seeking leader, everyday ministry exists as an avenue for performance. Ministry is done to build likes and subscriptions. It's a way to broadcast oneself. This means the leader's institutional commitment is only secure to the degree that the organization cooperates with his priority for self-expression.

The church, too, becomes repurposed and reshaped in the service of self. Origin stories are crafted, social media curated, an attractive persona circulated. Ministry is Kardashianized, with virtues shed or at least deprioritized because ministry life is shaped instead around self-promotion. In an ego-driven culture, networks exist, *not for my improvement, but for my platform.* And each time a celebrity pastor says, "I am the brand," the leader weakens the very platform they are seeking to build. It becomes one from which they will eventually topple.

Vice Audit 6: Egotism

Rank the degree to which you agree with the following statements on a scale of 1–5 (5 = strongly agree, 4 = agree, 3 = neutral, 2 = disagree, 1 = strongly disagree). Write your ranking in the blank to the left of each statement.

_____ 1. Many of our ministry efforts as a church focus on building the influence and platform of our key leader or leaders.

_____ 2. Our leaders live within their own "reality distortion field."

_____ 3. Our leaders have relational networks or small groups that create the illusion of honesty but supply little actual accountability.

_____ 4. For us, team has often been a revolving door. It's been difficult to keep good leaders.

_____ 5. The ambitions of our church have settled more exclusively on promoting our brand and don't often include promoting the greater kingdom good.

_____ **Total**

If your church and leadership scored between 0–8, you're likely cultivating a culture of humility. If you scored between 9–18, take some time to sit with your leadership team and talk through the marks of egotism in the chapter. If you scored between 19–25, your church is in danger of succumbing to the vice of egotism. Take some time to confess this to the Lord and begin praying that he will help you put off the selfish pursuit of a celebrity platform to humbly honor him.

Finally, an ego doesn't keep leaders. Attracting followers—even attracting other leaders—is part of the charm that makes a celebrity popular. But only good leaders keep leaders. When a leader's team is a revolving door, it typically means they don't play well in private. Collin Hansen once suggested to me that part of what separates great pastors from celebrities is the latter's inability to retain good help. In other words, a true measure of success is not merely attracting good men and women but also keeping those good people around.

I'm not necessarily talking here about the fallout from a disagreement or conflict. Build a church or a network of churches, and you can anticipate problems. Where there are people, there are problems. In conflict, sometimes things don't resolve, and people walk away. But one of the stunning similarities among fallen celebrity pastors is their penchant for showing the door to those who disagree. The egotistical leader often displays an unwillingness or inability to work through conflict. They either feel "above it," or they believe that exhibiting the character to work things through is beneath them.

If leaders around you or your network are leaving, look closely at why. Don't assume the blame lies entirely with them or with circumstantial issues external to you. Remember, egotistical pastors exist in their own Steve Jobs–style reality distortion bubble. So one way to be certain you are not courting celebrity is in your willingness to examine yourself or your own culpability. When other leaders see in us a humble willingness to suspect ourselves, this engenders trust.

Is Self-Glory the Axis of Your Ambitions?

What about you? Most of us will never have to negotiate the perils of real celebrity. We're not the kind of folks who can mesmerize a crowd with sparkling oration or brilliant insights. We're just ordinary leaders. But if social media has shown us anything, it's that the seed of egotism lies within all of us, just waiting to be watered by our own stupidity.

If social media has shown us anything, it's that the seed of egotism lies within all of us, just waiting to be watered by our own stupidity.

May God help us resist the temptation to seek celebrity and reaffirm our devotion to simple faithfulness. As Dietrich

Bonhoeffer once wrote, "The Church does not need brilliant personalities, but faithful servants of Jesus and the brethren."[7] That's why, whether you're a pastor, elder, or church planter, *the virtue of humility is essential.*

Think for a moment about how ambitions that have been bent toward egotism might affect your expectations for and experience with network leadership. In his epistle, James gives a sober assessment of what happens to a community when the wrong kind of ambition characterizes the culture:

> Who is wise and understanding among you? By his good conduct let him show his works in the meekness of wisdom. But if you have bitter jealousy and *selfish ambition* in your hearts, do not boast and be false to the truth. This is not the wisdom that comes down from above, but is earthly, unspiritual, demonic. For where jealousy and *selfish ambition* exist, there will be disorder and every vile practice (3:13–16, emphasis mine).

Selfish ambition is inordinate desire, glory seeking gone wrong. James says it's a symptom of the wrong kind of wisdom, the kind that disorders the soul and divides people from one another.

James wants us to look at our lives. When we do, what will we see? There are only two possible answers. We may see "wisdom from above," which is "pure, then peaceable, gentle, open to reason." This is the sort of character that creates a healthy culture for cultivating harmonious relationships (3:17–18).

The other option is that we'll see the sort of wisdom that is earthly and unspiritual (3:15). This wisdom is from below; it goes beyond nasty to demonic. When James says this, he's referencing the author of ambitions gone bad—Satan himself, the one who attempted to depose God and steal his glory. In other words, when self-glory is the axis of our ambitions, we repeat that first-ever coup attempt.

Interestingly, the original word James uses for "selfish ambition" denotes those who, like prostitutes or corrupt politicians, demean themselves for personal gain. It underscores the idea that we sell our soul in an attempt to grow bigger before others.

When self-glory is the axis of our ambitions, we repeat that first-ever coup attempt.

But the weight of self-exalting behavior collapses the scaffolding we build, and the debris and fallout pollute the community with whom we're connected.

John Chrysostom, one of the great preachers of the early church, once said, "Men who are in love with applause have their spirits starved . . . when they fail to be constantly praised."[8] Have you ever met people who are starving their souls in their search for praise? I have. In fact, I see one in the mirror all the time.

I've sought praise in meetings, subtly centering myself in the conversation or holding court with my ideas. I've caught glimpses of the disorder sometimes in my motive to preach, to pray, and to lead. When I'm on a quest for constant praise, I become an unconscious self-promoter. And in the process, I'm starving my soul. Thank God for Jesus and his finished work. He steps into my delusions of self-glory and moves my passions away from the praise of people and toward the glory that comes only from God (John 12:43).

My friends, the only hope for the future of networks and collectives is to grow more aware of this celebrity-seeking glory drive. We must act decisively when we see its evidence and believe the promise of James 4:10 (NIV): "Humble yourselves before the Lord, and he will lift you up."

Behold the Virtue: Humility

The first churches I served had humility-centered cultures. Some of the first messages I heard as a new believer were about that topic. Leaders wrote about humility and embodied it. It was regarded as an essential quality for any young person's leadership path. This was an encouragement-rich, self-reflective, conflict-resolving ministry world. In that context, I learned the value of correction, and I got better at discerning clear evidence of pride in my heart.

But the downside of this culture was that humility was sometimes taught—especially in the early days—without the gospel as the organizing center. Our teaching on humility (my own included) was connected not to the cross but to particular behaviors. As a result, humility took a distinct form and shape.

We also encouraged the softer expressions of humility. Our understanding of the virtue orbited around having an appearance of meekness and deference. We celebrated submission and unintentionally stigmatized humility's more rugged aspects.

For instance, we didn't emphasize the humility necessary for courageous dissent. We missed the reality that humble people sometimes say, "I'm willing to put your approval of me at risk by sharing my questions and reservations," or "I'm willing to take a stand here and be wrong."

The effect was that we functioned at that time in a spongy manner—more deferential and vulnerable to conformity. We created a caricature of what a humble person is like—one that many genuinely embraced but that others sought to emulate only outwardly. Since then, I think my old friends reformed some of these weaknesses. I pray I have as well. I think we've all learned that it's easy to conform to a set of celebrated behaviors while remaining arrogant in the heart.

As I've stepped out of that culture and into other networks, there are a few things I hope I've learned about humility—truths that may help your network leadership as well.

First, humility begins with an honest self-appraisal before God. Humility requires seeing ourselves as we really are in light of the reality of who God is. In fact, humility is nothing more than seeing reality clearly.

Humility is nothing more than seeing reality clearly.

What I like about this definition is that the focus is Godward, not *Me*-ward. Yes, I've got to look at myself, but only in comparison to the holy God who became human and suffered as our substitute. Ponder that, and it'll make you humble!

There's nothing about such humility that means we don't dream, aspire, and plan for great things. In fact, humility, biblically understood, should stoke a great ambition for new ways to bring God glory (see my fourth point below). But the ambition isn't oriented toward the self; it's oriented toward the Lord.

Did you ever notice how much harder it is for leaders of large churches to join partnerships? To be fair, we must acknowledge that their resources make it seem like certain needs are less *felt*. But these leaders are often unaccustomed to being in spaces where they are not leading. They may even prefer the role of being a provider of services. As a guy who led a large church for many years, my heart goes out to them. It takes humility for leaders of large churches to reconsider the self-appraisal boosted by their resources and to say of smaller church leaders, "I have need of you" (1 Corinthians 12:21). But the joy of doing mission alongside other churches—of being stronger together regardless of other churches' size, budget, or location—is something I long for leaders of large churches to experience.

Second, humility is cultivated through honest self-disclosure to others. Let's drop the illusion of having it all together. The only perfect man who walked this earth is Jesus. The rest of us are just bumbling through life until we discover what God already knows—that we are weak and sinful, and we still need Jesus every day.

Allow me to ask you a question—an important one for those who are leading large churches or even networks: When was the last time you confessed a sin to another person? Confession is important, not because it forces us to grovel, but because it acknowledges the reality of our brokenness, our humanity, and our daily need for grace.

When we confess our sins to one another, we find there is nothing we struggle with that is not common to man (1 Corinthians 10:13), and because we share common struggles at the deepest level, we also find comradery and deep fellowship with fellow believers. After all, we're *the community* of people who have found that the only solution for sin is God's just and faithful forgiveness. And because we confess our sins and receive God's forgiveness together as church communities, each church has a shared testimony.

Third, humility is ultimately measured by love. Jesus Christ's model in Philippians 2:1–11 is the ultimate standard of humility. You may know the context. The Philippians have an undercurrent of conceit and rivalry in their community that has resulted in division. So Paul first appeals to what every member of the community commonly shares in the gospel—encouragement in being united to Christ, comfort from his love, the shared presence of the Holy Spirit, as well as tenderness and compassion (2:1–2).

Next, Paul gives the church a double command: "Do nothing out of selfish ambition or vain conceit. Rather, in humility value others above yourselves" (2:3 NIV). Paul doesn't prescribe a set of behaviors for the Philippians; this is not a message on a dozen ways to be humble. Instead, he gives them a disposition. Given all they have in common, each Philippian member *must count the others as more significant* than themselves. He's telling them, "Take the focus off yourself and make much of others. Count them to be more important!" He doesn't want them to fight for unity and humility by preoccupying themselves with rooting out pride in one another but by pouring themselves out in service to one another. For Paul, it's *love* that becomes the slayer of pride and exhibits the best evidence of humility.

In *Mere Christianity*, C. S. Lewis writes about what we experience when we meet a truly humble person:

> Probably all you will think about him is that he seemed a cheerful, intelligent chap who took a real interest in what *you* said to *him*. If you do dislike him it will be because you feel a little envious of anyone who seems to enjoy life so easily. He will not be thinking about humility: he will not be thinking about himself at all.[9]

This is where Rick Warren and Tim Keller get their concept of humility as "self-forgetfulness."[10] The first time I heard Keller use that term, I thought he was nuts! But I was thinking about it through my old paradigm. Humble people don't necessarily think less of themselves; they think about themselves less, because they're thinking about how to show love to you!

Finally, humility should not hinder ambition. Our desire to be humble shouldn't make us reluctant to speak about aspirations. When I wrote my book *Rescuing Ambition*, one of the first things I discovered was that Christians don't typically write on the subject.[11] That may seem noble, but I've concluded that it's dangerous. Alexis de Tocqueville had the same concern about humanity in general:

> What worries me most is the danger that, amid all the constant trivial preoccupations of private life, ambition may lose both its force and its greatness, that human passions may grow gentler and at the same time baser, with the result that the progress of the body social may become daily quieter and less aspiring.[12]

For Tocqueville, the words *ambition* and *aspiration* function as synonyms. Now go read the qualifications for an elder in 1 Timothy 3! The first one listed is an aspiration for the office. Without ambition, new strategies aren't explored, churches aren't planted, and nations aren't reached. Without ambition, we'd have no Christian ministers.

We can't sacrifice ambition in pursuit of humility or set them up as if they are opposed. We don't need Christians who are so modest they aspire to nothing.

We can't sacrifice ambition in pursuit of humility or set them up as if they are opposed. We don't need Christians who are so modest they aspire to nothing. Humility will often harness our ambition, but it shouldn't hinder it.

Behold the Son!

What is the most remarkable and distinctive thing about Jesus? His popularity? No. There have been plenty of popular religious leaders who have been known the world over. His amazing power? Maybe—he certainly had plenty of it. His incredible wisdom? It *was* mind-boggling. His exemplary character? Perhaps—after all, he was perfect! But of all these things, the apostle Paul points the Philippians to one word: *humility*. Read it again with me:

> Do nothing out of selfish ambition or vain conceit. Rather, in humility value others above yourselves, not looking to your own interests but each of you to the interests of the others.
>
> In your relationships with one another, have the same mindset as Christ Jesus:
>
> Who, being in very nature God,
>> did not consider equality with God something to
>>> be used to his own advantage;
> rather, he made himself nothing
>> by taking the very nature of a servant,
>> being made in human likeness.
> And being found in appearance as a man,
>> he humbled himself
>> by becoming obedient to death—
>>> even death on a cross! (Philippians 2:3–8 NIV)

This passage is part of a letter to leaders whom Paul loved—leaders in his network and with whom he celebrated a strong partnership (1:3–5, 8). As he writes, he prays for them (1:9), and the advance of the gospel is foremost in his mind (1:5, 27). But like all churches, Philippi has its share of colorful personalities and problems. Later, in chapter 4, Paul mentions two ladies—Euodia and Syntyche—who seem to have public disagreements. Their conflict seems typical of a broader disunity within the church. Selfish ambition is working its divisive magic.

So Paul put before that church what is perhaps the greatest paradox ever: God Almighty—who is right and good and worthy to seek his own celebrity—in humility. He shows us the direction biblical ambition points, the way Jesus himself traveled, the direction our churches and networks must go— namely, *down.*

When we truly understand what Christ accomplished through his incarnation, death, and resurrection—the incalculable love displayed in his atoning sacrifice—then we clearly see the power that both humbles us and keeps us humble. As we empty ourselves, we step away from our ego and find the fullness of Christ. We adopt an honest self-appraisal, embrace real accountability, and step out in ambitious love. We follow Christ, who had the acclaim of heaven but made himself nothing for our sakes. In his steps, we can confidently humble ourselves and build networks and denominations anchored to the promise:

> This is the one to whom I will look:
>> he who is humble and contrite in spirit
>> and trembles at my word. (Isaiah 66:2)

VIRTUE

MODESTY

Against Triumphalism

My dad was a steelworker in Pittsburgh, as was his father before him, and his grandfather as well. I worked in a steel mill for one summer during college and vowed never to return. I never did.

Imagine a world where everything—from tools to toilet seats—remains caked with soot. Then jack up the temperature to 110 degrees, cover your entire body with protective clothing (also smothered in soot), and populate the workforce with hungover people who don't want to be there. That's my memory of the steel mill. *Nothing* improved my college grades more than my fear of returning to one.

Dad worked in the steel mill for twenty-nine years.

My father was a Navy guy who returned from the Korean War to get married and start a family. I guess he was a family man, at least in the way it was defined back in the '60s and '70s. Dad worked hard, loved his wife, modeled determination, provided for his kids, dutifully attended church twice a year, and vacationed religiously at the Jersey shore.

I'm not sure whether the trees came before the steel mill or because of the steel mill, but my dad loved trees. He would arrive home from work and escape immediately into the yard

153

to prune, spray, dig, and tend. When I close my eyes, I can see him happily digging a hole with a near-perfect circumference while a burlap-sacked sapling was perched near the rim. A tree whisperer in mill-hunks clothing.

Trees were dad's sanctuary—a place of rejuvenation, a place where he nurtured life. On his days off, he worked tirelessly in the yard, trousers resting low enough to display the upper half of his backside. He was too busy cultivating what would become the greenest quarter acre in all of Pittsburgh to care for.

Once, as a small boy, I remember buying a tree for my dad. Long before love languages were a thing, I knew the loudest statement of esteem one could make to my father was a tree. I bought a maple, or maybe a birch—who knows. When you're nine years old, they all look the same. My dad acted like he had won the lottery. Into the yard he went, spade in hand, tearing into Mother Earth like he knew where the gold was buried. It wasn't until I was older that I realized trees were living things he cultivated outside of the darkness of where he worked. Soot was death; trees were *life*.

My bus stop was down the road, so I walked past the tree on school days for years to come. Under Dad's care, the tree grew from seedling to sapling, eventually spreading its limbs wide toward maturity. In the shade of its branches, the mill-worker toiled happily to strengthen the tree's life and postpone its decline. As the youngest kid in our family, I was a quiet observer of the long and fruitful process.

When I see a tree being planted, I sometimes think about my dad. But now I also think about the places where his experience with trees overlaps with what I've learned about churches and movements. Little did I know that by watching a steelworker tend trees, I would learn so much about churches and the networks that unite them.

The Wood Wide Web

Trees form a remarkable analogy for our efforts in the exhilarating world of missional movement and network development. Planting trees requires hard work and resources. To thrive, trees need each other. When planted close together in a forest, they form relationships that naturally synchronize with one another. The entire forest is fed by *mycorrhizas*[1]—a symbiotic relationship between trees, fungi, dead wood, and a whole lot of underground stuff that ensures nutrients are transferred to a web of trees.[2] Trees cluster to share resources. They are stronger together.

Trees also reproduce. They have remarkable ways of adapting to their environment so they can multiply. Many varieties can reproduce by breaking off a portion of the tree—a cutting—and replanting it elsewhere. When this happens, the new trees become a carbon copy of the tree from which the cutting was taken.

Trees sustain life. They grab carbon dioxide molecules from the air, use the sun's energy, and produce the air we breathe. Trees also provide a home. Half of all the creatures on this globe make their home in or on trees.

Every tree on earth shares one final similarity. After a life of living, growing, supplying, and replicating, each tree will die. In death, they decay into environments that ultimately sow life back into standing trees[3]—or become the desk in front of me or the bookshelves to my right. "No other part of this planet's ecosystem," observes Matthew Sleeth, "has so much utility both in life and in death."[4]

Think about it. Trees are planted, sustain life, provide homes, reproduce, live interdependently, and even in dying continue to bear fruit—just like networks.

Trees are planted, sustain life, provide homes, reproduce, live interdependently, and even in dying continue to bear fruit—just like networks.

Behold the Virtue: Modesty

When I consider the impact of one small slice of creation—trees—I am amazed and humbled. It makes me think of how God moves in churches and networks. Sure, we can plant, cultivate, protect, reproduce, and monitor the ecosystem. But like the flourishing of a tree, so much of the process is outside of our control. I think that's why pastors, networks, and movement leaders need modesty.

When I talk about modesty, I'm not referencing midriffs and yoga pants. The definition of *modesty* derives from *modus*, a Latin word meaning "measure, manner, or mood." Modesty expresses how we think and speak about ourselves. Modest leaders aren't out to grab attention by flaunting their abilities or assets. They make their manner worthy of the gospel (Philippians 1:27; 2:5–11) by adopting a humble and unassuming posture. The modest leader does not overestimate their abilities or overcommunicate their impact. In fact, when communicating, the modest leader will make much of Jesus and much of others, beginning with those overlooked and undervalued by society (1 Corinthians 12:23).

A great synonym for modesty is *meekness* (2 Corinthians 10:1; Colossians 3:12; James 3:13). Great antonyms—or opposites—are *hype*, *fruit demanding*, and *legacy keeping*. Important things happen in the culture of a network or movement when we sow the virtue of modesty.

First, sowing modesty moves our message away from hype and toward Jesus. Hype is exaggerated promotion or publicity. For the network or denominational leader, it's the evil that crouches at the door of every mission update, ministry overview, and phone call with prospective planters or churches. I hate confessing this to you, but I've hyped myself more times than I care to admit. You know what I mean. We exaggerate our organizational strengths so they appear as though they're on steroids—as if the apostle Paul himself were leading the ministry. The *hype hijack* at work in our hearts converts reality into idealism.

Don't get me wrong. I'm not suggesting we undersell God's activity in the name of modesty. I'm just saying that we should not oversell it in the hope that it will make us look better than we are. Paul's modesty among the Corinthians is seen through his sharing of his weaknesses. In fact, his weaknesses were his defense, even his boast, because God's "power is made perfect in weakness." (2 Corinthians 12:9). We know we're moving away from the hype hijack when our portrayals of our group include our weaknesses.

As the recently appointed president of our network of churches, I had the opportunity to address the network's pastors at a conference. It was just a few months into my tenure, and this was the first time I was meeting many of them. By the grace of God, representatives from most of our churches and most of the countries were in attendance.

I knew it was customary for a new leader to cast a provocative vision for the future, but I've learned from my mistakes. When you are dealing with thinking leaders, it's better to aim for modesty. Plus, these guys were embattled and principled leaders. They would sniff out hype a mile away.

So I told them that what we are seeking to accomplish together would not be easy. Partnerships are complicated. I reminded them that better folks than we are have stood helpless as their networks or denominations dissolved right before their eyes. I told them it's unlikely that we, even with our best collaborative efforts, will discover all the secrets of interdependence that have somehow eluded other groups in history. "We are average people with modest gifts," I said, "and partnerships will teach us that we are even more average than we imagined." In my experience, the only thing harder than partnerships is parenting—and both involve a lot of whining.

To close out the address, we fled together to the gospel! I exhorted them to not forget the One we follow. He is not a leader but the Savior—the One who loved us, died for us, and began a good work in us. And God the Father will bring his work to completion in the day of Christ Jesus (Philippians 1:6).

Why settle for hype when we have a real hero to celebrate!

I listened to a *New York Times* bestselling audiobook recently in which the author exclaimed, "I am my own hero." He then urged others to adopt the same view. For the gospel movement leader, that idea—so enticing to the modern mind—is the problem, not the solution.

The "I'm the hero" hype is hardwired into our hearts from birth. But the modest way is to look outside of ourselves. In fact, the churches and networks we treasure are valuable only to the degree that they point toward and celebrate the ultimate Hero who was "crucified in weakness, but lives by the power of God" (2 Corinthians 13:4). It is literally impossible to speak of Jesus with hype hijacking the conversation. We just don't have the knowledge, or the vocabulary, to accurately exalt the glory and magnificence of his person and work.

> *The "I'm the hero" hype is hardwired into our hearts from birth. But the modest way is to look outside of ourselves.*

Second, sowing modesty helps us trust God with his timing for fruitfulness. Modesty should not soften the soul or make us less aspiring. Our modesty should be seen in our self-appraisal, not in our efforts for God or our prayers for what might be accomplished. Modesty carries a mirror. It's about how we see self, not what we believe about God. "Modesty," said G. K.

Chesterton, "has moved from the organ of ambition. Modesty has settled upon the organ of conviction; where it was never meant to be. A man was meant to be doubtful about himself, but undoubting about the truth; this has been exactly reversed."[5]

Holding up the mirror of modesty, we get to work. In other words, modesty persuades us of our need for progress and production. In a sense, a modest look in the mirror inspires great aspirations for God's glory. For network pastors and leaders, the modesty of the heart is seen in how fully and wholeheartedly they are given to gospel growth.

When modesty informs our self-appraisal, it influences our expectations around the effect of our efforts. Modesty attacks the entitlement that says, "By now, God should have delivered this kind of fruit in our church or network." I'm not questioning, mind you, whether there should be fruit from our labors. I'm merely suggesting that modesty does not hold God hostage to the timing of fruitfulness. For this reason, Paul was able to say, "I do not account my life of any value nor as precious to myself, if only I may finish my course and the ministry that I received from the Lord Jesus, to testify to the gospel of the grace of God" (Acts 20:24).

Paul's measure for the value of his life and gifts was evidenced in his faithfulness to testify about the gospel. No mention of the number of churches he planted or served, just the sense that some things are so worthy that mere obedience is enough. Some goals are so glorious that just being faithful is enough. When or how the fruit blooms are the prerogative of wise and loving providence.

Telling Stories of Loss

The church where I pastored in the Philadelphia area for twenty-eight years once planted a church not far from our own building. Planting the church was a godly man, his praying wife, some wonderful kids, and a solid core team. The church was bathed in prayer and support as they encountered an astonishing array of risks and costs.

Like all church planters, this guy sacrificially served—preaching, shepherding, praying, and navigating the complexities of pastoring in an urban area. But as one year led into another, the discernable fruit of viability and vitality just didn't come. After five years, the church closed.

On the final Sunday, the church held a banquet after the final service had concluded. While they ate together, the members testified to God's activity and celebrated his goodness over the past five years. Then as the banquet came to an end—and the history of that church ended—one man stood up and began to sing words from a familiar song: "Thank you for the cross. Thank you, Lord, for drawing me . . . Thank you, Lord, for saving me. Haven't you been good!"[6]

As the man's singing echoed around the banquet room, a holy conviction settled on the people. One after another, all around the room, they began to sing, earnestly joining with voices that truly believed the substance of the song. Through their five years together, God was good. Through dangers, toils, and snares, God was good. Though the church was closing, God was *still* good.

While the pastor sat beholding this holy moment, he realized an important truth I hope is sealed in the heart of every leader reading this book: *Some goals are so worthy that it's glorious to even make the attempt.*

Some goals are so worthy that it's glorious to even make the attempt.

If you're leading in network or denominational life, let me offer a couple of applications.

First, make sure all church planters know they are heroes. Whether the planted church galvanizes quickly or especially if the planter's efforts don't yield the intended fruit, make it clear that every church planter is a hero. It takes the same courage, work, prayer, and effort to plant a church that falters as it does to plant a church that grows. In fact, one could make the case that ending a church takes even more courage and prayer since that planter must engage in the heartwrenching evaluation process that results in the decision to shut the doors.

We all know that planters with churches where growth is slow or stalled tend to get overlooked or ignored at the big network and denominational events. Their stories are often overlooked in the updates and highlights. Church planting families in this situation already live under the specter of failure. Sadly, our silence magnifies the shame.

I'm not trying to make a case for low expectations. Let's limit painful closings through rigorous assessment and training, as well as through faithful support and care. But the reality is that church plants falter in every network. In a fallen world, no ministry scores 100 percent on every multiplication effort. If they did, why would they need God?

Second, pull the stories of loss out of the closet. Tell these stories. To do so not only dignifies the planter, but it also mines the lessons of loss. Let the network see how you treat those who don't satisfy your hopes and expectations. Let them see into your network's organizational soul through the compassionate way you talk about plants that never grew. Few things fortify a culture more quickly—for good or ill—than watching how leaders relate to people who do not bear the anticipated fruit (Luke 15:11–32; John 7:53–8:11).

Beware the Vice: Triumphalism

Watching my dad tend trees over the years convinced me of the unalterable reality that trees die. Some live long, growing an inner circle of rings that tell their age; others decay unexpectedly. Eventually even those trees that are grown under the best conditions and tended with the most experienced hand die.

This brings us to a delicate part of our journey, a place where I say some things that may be hard to accept. But to be a good leader, we must honestly face these realities and think them through. We must embrace a modesty that helps us to *plant, build, and love ministries that will not last.*

Just as trees die, so churches, networks, and denominations also die. That's bracing to hear, I know. Most folks aren't thinking beyond the next ministry season. Others carry a long-term vision, just assuming their present role is unalterable. Still others—and this is quite often the vice of organizational leaders—want their labors to result in timeless monuments here on earth.

The vice of *triumphalism* feasts on a significance that modesty denies. Let's call it the idol of *immortality*—the longing to convert ministry into some enduring earthly namesake by which we will be remembered and celebrated. Networks and church leaders who begin to worship at this altar abandon modesty in at least three ways.

> The vice of triumphalism feasts on a significance that modesty denies.

First, triumphalism forsakes historical sobriety. When we allow church history to inform our sense of significance, our lust for immortality is sobered. As the Lord says in Jeremiah 6:16, "Stand at the crossroads and look; ask for the ancient paths, ask where the good way is, and walk in it, and you will find rest for your souls" (NIV). In other words, when the past brings perspective to the present, it also produces rest!

When history is lost as a reference point, the significance we give to our own place in time soars. Each generation tends to see its own era as a watershed moment. We galvanize with urgency because the days have never been so dark, the burning needs so imperative, the past church so misguided. The passionate superiority of our cause mobilizes us with feverish zeal. It all feels so monumental, so very historically exceptional.

Honestly, when a person is involved in a church plant or a new gospel movement, it is often a life-transforming experience. I treasure memories of being part of both. But my youthful sense that our movement was embodying something peerless and permanent said more about my heart than God's intention. Being part of something new did not mean being part of something better. Without history, I lacked modesty.

History humbles us. It tutors us downward, grounding our longing for significance in the soil of modesty. It helps us avoid what C. S. Lewis called "chronological snobbery"—the uncritical assumption that whatever has gone out of date is obviously irrelevant.[7] In 1 Kings 12, King Rehoboam rejected the wisdom of older men, believing they were outdated and irrelevant. The younger leaders, his friends, had new ideas. He thought old was bad and new was good. But it led to disaster and Israel's rejection of his leadership.

In the 1970s and '80s, cutting-edge Christians adopted contemporary worship music, which put aside old hymns for a more "vibrant" personal faith, and built churches around the felt needs of target demographics (the homogeneous unit principle). These leaders believed these methods were the way forward for church planting. Their heart in these efforts was to reach people with the gospel, and it worked!

But the Gen X and Millennial children who were reached by that Boomer generation have now (with many legitimate reasons) rejected both these ideas—reclaiming the ancient faith of old hymns (and even the liturgies) and pursuing diverse, multicultural churches as an apologetic for biblical justice. It makes you wonder what generational faults are at work right now that will soon be uncovered by the future Gen Alpha leaders who are shaping Play-Doh in our children's ministries. What are we blind to until their labor opens our eyes?

It's a common practice today for people of various tribal and political stripes to indulge in pronouncing that those with whom they disagree are on "the wrong side of history." I believe this is an egregious example of chronological snobbery. Implied in this verdict is the conviction, "My side is right; your side salutes Nazis." History, then, is not a professor who nurtures modesty but a weapon we wield to ridicule.

Jesus was on the wrong side of history until morning broke on day three, post-crucifixion. Then Jesus flipped to the right side of history—or I guess it would be more accurate to say that history flipped over to his side. That divide in the ages should be a warning to us. We should be careful not to sentence one another as if we own the best take on the past. After all, the tectonic plates of history can shift in a day. God wants us on Christ's side of history, whether the historians approve or not.

That's the problem with triumphalism. It confines us to the voices of our own age; it tempts us toward institutional arrogance, which is a shortcut to irrelevant institutionalism. Historical sobriety by contrast opens our souls to be shaped by those whose thinking and labors have passed the test of time.

The best car I ever owned was a 1972 Chrysler Valiant. My wife, Kimm, called it the "Wonder V," as in, "I wonder why you think I want to ride in that." But it was a tank on tires—so solidly built that I used it as a backstop for tossing baseballs. A baseball into the side of my present car would total it. But the Wonder V seemed unstoppable. Desolate was the day it gave up the ghost. After all, when something is solid, well-built, and passes the test of time, we need to value it.

That's the way we need to understand church planting strategies. In a world where new gets the buzz, we need to value that which has proven itself over time. I've already shared that I was part of a family of churches that has been planting churches for more than three decades. But from a historical perspective, we were just little pups. We had the well-earned reputation for being as slow as my Valiant. Much of that was because we wanted to build well. But we also learned something: for us to move forward, we needed the past.

It starts, of course, with the biblical models we've been exploring in Philippians and the book of Acts. But after the Scriptures, we need to study church planting as it has been carried out in history. You won't find the Apostolic Fathers talking about church planting, but churches have been planted for two millennia. We must look at how John Calvin and Martin Luther and the early Reformers re-created the church in local contexts at the dawn of the Protestant era. We need to see how the experiments in church planting that occurred among Puritans and pilgrims worked and didn't work. We may be in the first or second generation to carve out a specific practical theology for church planting, but as with everything else, someone has worked the field before us.

Here's an example. Did you know that Charles Spurgeon had a church planting movement? The Metropolitan Tabernacle didn't just feature great numbers of members; it was a church planting church. Perhaps the most significant auxiliary work of Pastors' College (founded in 1856 and renamed Spurgeon's

College in 1923)—that which made the greatest long-lasting contribution—was the work done in church planting. Scores of churches were planted in London, throughout Britain, and the world because of the efforts of the college's students.

Learning history nurtures historical sobriety—and with men like Spurgeon as our model—this won't mean sacrificing urgency. To reach our communities and entrust the gospel to the next generation, we must plant churches.

Second, triumphalism ignores the decline of life. This is the hard news. Churches have life cycles.[8] They are born, they live to bear fruit, and almost each one dies. J. Robert Clinton estimates the life cycle of a church in the Western world to be about five generations. It matters little whether the exact number is more or less. The point stands that churches die. Think about it. The churches the apostles planted are gone. The church that Jesus' brother led is gone. Great churches throughout history? All gone.

It's true of great institutions too. I recently heard Albert Mohler say that only three institutions have lasted more than a thousand years: the Roman Catholic Church, the British Parliament, and eight medieval universities.[9] That's it.

It brings me no happiness to be the bearer of this news, but the church in which you labor may not be around in the future. The more we want our network to bear our name and imprint, the quicker it ends. Your group was not designed to bear your glory. It was created for the glory of another—and death seems to be a hidden truth behind what animates his glory and moves his work forward.

Triumphalism dulls our sense for discerning decline. The walls of our work must be glossed with good news. Decay is overlooked and renewal is assumed. *Of course our work will live on!*

Sometimes pastors think that all of God's promises to preserve the *universal church* apply to their *local church* as an organization. Dedicated Christian leaders have wandered the world planting churches and starting Christian organizations with the expectation that these labors would live on—must live on—for God's work to continue. John Calvin once observed, "We undertake all things as if we were establishing immortality for ourselves on earth."[10] But tucked within the folds of that desire is often a desire to build large and indestructible monuments to our own significance. It's a veiled quest for immortality.[11]

Such dreams for immortality blind us to the reality that a bloody death lies at the center of our faith. Throughout history, the pathway to the future has always passed through the valley of the shadow: "Unless a grain of wheat falls into the earth and dies, it remains alone; but if it dies, it bears much fruit" (John 12:24).

How is this reality landing on you? It's important for us to recalibrate. The universal church that Christ is building is eternal. The particular ministries we lead? Well, not so much. But what if you're here long enough to save souls, bear fruit, serve one another, and transfer your mission into the hands of the next generation? Is that enough? Or is your longing more akin to the lust for legacy ascribed to Alexander Hamilton in the Broadway musical: "God help and forgive me. I wanna build something that's gonna outlive me."[12]

History gives us a clear picture of what to expect. Our church may outlive us. Some work does outlive its laborers—but even that is temporary. Our churches ultimately exist to point to things that are eternal.

When leaders come to terms with the reality of an unbounded mission within a finite local church, it purifies our motivation for planting and leading. Our grasp of mortality confines our efforts to the things over which we have some degree of control—namely, reaching the living lost who need Christ and then prudently passing the baton to the next generation. But a hundred years from now? For most of us, no one—save God—will ever know we existed. Is that enough?

Third, triumphalism can overlook seasons of fertility. If churches have life cycles, as all living things do, then let's not sit around grieving our shelf life. Let's celebrate our season of fertility and look to aggressively reproduce churches while we are in the best position to do so.

Multiplication is what we must do to entrust the gospel to the next generation (2 Timothy 2:2).

This news should leave us with a fresh urgency to plant churches while our local church or network is still capable and fruitful. Remember, church planting is an act of renewal. The sacrifice required to pursue mission contributes a vital nutrient into the bloodstream of your church; it helps your church last longer.

As a lead pastor, I discovered that my fears about church planting were largely unfounded. My dread over the impact of sacrificing teams or planters was met by our faithful God, who resupplies our needs and fuels our church with fresh vision. Each time I stood on the stage to send out another team and thought, *Will we ever recover?* God showed me that recovery was too small a goal. He designed sending to help us thrive! I learned that church planting is like an oil change; it extends the life of the church's engine by stoking the renewal dynamics necessary for ongoing flourishing.

My friends, the time to plant churches is now. The time to disciple the next generation of planters is now; the time to accept your mortality and build a multiplying church is now;

the time to start new networks is now too. Give yourself in the present to extend the fame of the only name that triumphs—the name of Jesus!

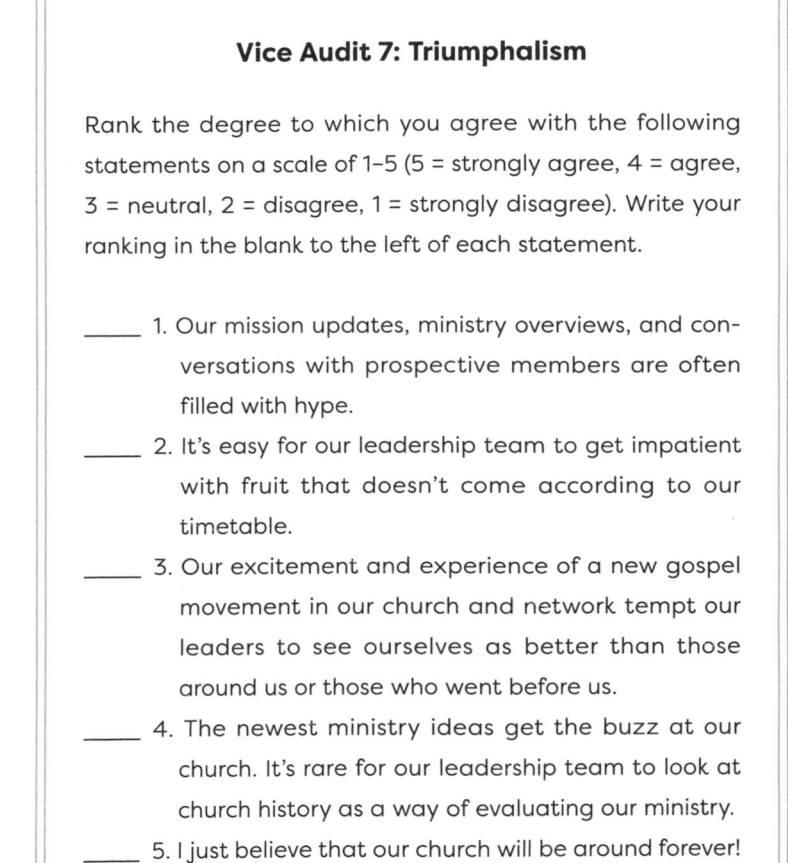

Vice Audit 7: Triumphalism

Rank the degree to which you agree with the following statements on a scale of 1–5 (5 = strongly agree, 4 = agree, 3 = neutral, 2 = disagree, 1 = strongly disagree). Write your ranking in the blank to the left of each statement.

_____ 1. Our mission updates, ministry overviews, and conversations with prospective members are often filled with hype.

_____ 2. It's easy for our leadership team to get impatient with fruit that doesn't come according to our timetable.

_____ 3. Our excitement and experience of a new gospel movement in our church and network tempt our leaders to see ourselves as better than those around us or those who went before us.

_____ 4. The newest ministry ideas get the buzz at our church. It's rare for our leadership team to look at church history as a way of evaluating our ministry.

_____ 5. I just believe that our church will be around forever!

_____ **Total**

If your church and leadership scored between 0–8, you're likely cultivating a culture of modesty. If you scored between 9–18, take some time to sit with your leadership

> team and talk through the characteristics of triumphalist leaders described in the chapter. If you scored between 19–25, your church is in danger of succumbing to the vice of triumphalism. Take some time to confess this to the Lord and begin praying that he will help you cultivate a culture of contentment and modest expectations.

The Gospel and Immortality

If you see yourself in this quest for immortality, you're not alone. I can relate. I've built some monuments and lived long enough to see them topple. The older I get, the more I assume that my best motives are mixed. "Our best works are shot through with sin," said J. I. Packer, "and contain something that needs to be forgiven."[13] Even in the writing of this book, there is, quite honestly, an undeniable desire that my words and work will be remembered long after I am gone. The war against triumphalism rages within my own heart.

What should network leaders tell themselves when their desire for immortality exerts supremacy over their delight in modesty? How does the gospel help all of us vanquish this vice? Here are four final encouragements:

First, when we find our distinction in what we do, we must remember what Christ has done. The gospel brings me explosive news. My search for approval is over. In Christ, I already have all the approval I need. Because Christ's righteousness has been transferred to me, all the time and energy I squander trying to be praised or celebrated or to build a legacy to validate my existence can now be redirected toward doing things for God's glory.

Christ's record of perfect obedience now frames God's

vision of my existence. When God looks at me, he no longer sees me wallowing in my naked grabs for glory. He sees the riches of Christ's obedience in life and death. I no longer live and lead *for* approval; I live and lead *from* approval.

Second, as we confess our immodest motives, the gospel restructures our affections. The gospel is not a stagnant compilation of data. It's not merely a message, but it is the power of God—a dynamic force unleashed within creation (Romans 1:16). Because Jesus died and rose for us, we have real power to break free from a life and a way of leading consumed by self. Jesus' self-giving life teaches that life is more than me. The gospel rightsizes our self-estimation by reminding us that we are dearly loved but deeply sinful. Our role is not a place for us to perform or build a platform, but an opportunity to display Christ's love, exercise God's gifts, and pursue good deeds among the church and toward the world. The gospel reminds us that because God first loved us, we can love our family, our church, and the world as ourselves. Remember, God knows all (Psalm 139:1–4), and he evaluates you lovingly and graciously, not by your triumphs, but in light of his success on the cross (Colossians 1:11–12).

Third, though we encounter vices in the church on earth, we can rejoice because this world is not our home. Where there are people, there are problems. People are human; they disappoint. We're tempted to grow cynical. We feel defrauded by God because of the differences we detect between what the church is and what she ought to be.

But our churches were never meant to be heaven. In fact, our dwelling here is only temporary (2 Peter 3:13). We have no abiding city here (Hebrews 13:14). Christ's completed work has earned us a place with God forever (John 19:30). When we arrive safely home in the new heaven and the new earth, we will see God's church—complete with virtues and vices—through the eyes of eternity; and we will stand amazed at how God used all of it for his glory (Isaiah 65:17; Revelation 21:1–7).

Jesus doesn't promise us an answer to every question, nor does he promise to take away the suffering, griefs, and pains of leadership. But Jesus does offer us something eternal today— the comfort of his love and presence, his rest and refuge. He offers us a secure identity and the certainty of his promises. Sure, networks are hard. But Jesus is greater, and you will soon see him face-to-face.

Fourth and finally, when we feel the fragility and impermanence of our work, we can rest (and work) in light of Jesus' unchanging refuge. Planting churches and building networks bring complexity, but the problems are never random. In the midst of the complexity, God works in and through us. Because of Jesus, we wake up each day to new mercies (Lamentations 3:22–23) as new creations (2 Corinthians 5:17). We can rejoice, whatever our circumstances (Psalm 136:1–26; Philippians 4:4). In God, we're promised stable refuge in the midst of today's crisis (Psalm 91:1–16; Philippians 4:7), as well as endurance for the future (John 17:1–26; Jude 24).

We don't need to build a permanent monument to our existence. Christ is building his church for his eternal glory, and we have been invited into *that* adventure! Whether our names are remembered on earth are inconsequential because God has written them in his book of life (Luke 10:20; Philippians 4:3).

Even Trees Die, But the God's Work through Partnership Endures

No one who plants a tree believes it will live forever. If they've done their homework, they know that while it lives, it may bear fruit, beautify the space it inhabits, produce oxygen for breathing, pass along nitrogen to other plants, reproduce by scattering seeds, and form a web of interdependence with other trees in a forest.

But trees are not eternal; they have life cycles. While they live, they thrive by supplying life to things outside of themselves. When it comes to interdependence, trees give far more than they take. They are remarkably productive for something that spends a lifetime standing in the same place.

The same can be true for our churches and networks. We should be modest and sober about the truth that they will not last into eternity. Yet, amazingly, we can believe that the message we preach and the lives we influence are changed for eternity.

With Jesus Christ as our ultimate refuge, we can move forward with wise urgency.

Dear leader, please remember that you and your church will one day die. So while there is time—while our churches and networks are fertile and there is strength within us—push forward on mission. Don't do it to build your brand or stroke the immortality idol. After all, we don't know what tomorrow holds. But we do know who holds tomorrow.

For the glory of his name and the spread of his fame, let's be on mission to plant churches, knowing that as we go with him and for him, we are stronger together!

ACKNOWLEDGMENTS

I t takes a village to write a book. Let me introduce you to the community of friends, family, and counselors who helped bring this project to print.

First, thank you to my friends leading networks who agreed to review and interact with the ideas—Dave Owens from Harbor Network, Clint Clifton from Pillar Network, and Daniel Yang from Send Institute. "Iron sharpens iron, and one man sharpens another" (Proverbs 27:17). Thank you for the sparks.

The innovators at Catapult—Todd, Doug, and Andy—came through in a huge way as we collaborated on the Network Matrix. Andy Graham was also kind enough to review the book and drop serious insights. If you are confronting network complexity, get to know these guys. Hats off to Catapult!

Ryan Pazdur and the team at Zondervan displayed kindness and gracious flexibility toward me as this project played out against the backdrop of a family tragedy. Thank you, Ryan.

Jared Kennedy and I have partnered together as editor and writer for many years. Recently he took an editing role at The Gospel Coalition, and, well, I already feel the gaping void. Jared, I thank God for our friendship and for the way your many gifts made my voice more decipherable.

The board of Great Commission Collective and my wonderful GCC team provided vocal and unrelenting encouragement as I undertook and completed this project. I'm deeply grateful for our partnership in the gospel. I happen to love our friendships too. Thank you.

Kimm—not to mention my entire family—has been a constant support in my writing efforts. In moments like this, a mere thank you seems so insufficient. But for now, it must do. *Thank you.*

I treasure my experiences of leading and loving within Sovereign Grace Ministries and Sojourn Network. May God richly bless the new iterations of his gracious gospel work within us all.

NOTES

Introduction

1. Dave Harvey, *The Plurality Principle: How to Build and Maintain a Thriving Church Leadership Team* (Wheaton, IL: Crossway, 2021).

Virtue 1: Conviction

1. John Piper, *Let the Nations Be Glad: The Supremacy of God in Missions* (Grand Rapids: Baker Academic, 2010), 182.
2. George W. Peters, *A Biblical Theology of Missions* (Chicago: Moody, 1972), 178.
3. I'm grateful to Chris Bruno and Matt Dirks for this insight drawn from their thoughtful book titled *Churches Partnering Together: Biblical Strategies for Fellowship, Evangelism, and Compassion* (Wheaton, IL: Crossway, 2014), 27.
4. Thomas Nettles says, "The Baptist . . . view of the autonomy of the local congregation has caused numerous difficulties in maintaining the full cooperation of its many local congregations in a united action for missions" ("Baptists and the Great Commission" in *The Great Commission*, eds. Martin I. Klauber and Scott M. Manetsch [Nashville: Broadman & Holman, 2008], 102).
5. Eckhard J. Schnabel wrote, "The majority of Paul's coworkers came from the new churches that the apostle had established. Some of them came to Paul as 'delegates' from their home churches (Colossians 1:7; 4:12–13; Philemon 13); they represent their churches as *apostoloi ekklesion* (2 Corinthians 8:23; cf. Philippians 2:25) and have a responsibility as servants of the larger body of Christ to build up the kingdom of God. Their participation in Paul's mission makes

up what their churches owe to Paul (1 Corinthians 16:17; Philippians 2:30). The churches participate through their envoys in Paul's mission. Wolfgang Schrage is correct when he observes that the role of the coworkers 'cannot be determined only along psychological lines on the basis of the need for fellowship, nor along organizational lines in terms of maximizing the missionary effectiveness, nor along pedagogical lines in terms of training workers for the time after Paul. Rather, Paul emphasizes the co-responsibility and the participation of the churches because he regards missionary work and ministry as a function of the entire church (thus the great fluctuation in his team of coworkers)'" (*Early Christian Mission: Paul and The Early Church* [Downers Grove, IL: InterVarsity, 2004], 1441).

6. George Peters noted, "The independence of the local church is beautifully balanced by the interdependence of the churches . . . Indeed, no one liveth to himself, not even the local church. There is strength in the proper mobilization and coordination of our interdependence which results in unity of purpose and action. This needs to be emphasized again and again. Individualism asserts itself not only in the individual but also in the absolutization of the independence and autonomy of the local church" (*Biblical Theology of Missions*, 225).

7. Paraphrasing Joseph Fitzmyer, quoted in Robert L. Plummer, "A Theological Basis for the Church's Mission in Paul," *Westminster Theological Journal* 64, no. 2 (Fall 2002): 258, n. 20.

8. Bruno and Dirks, *Churches Partnering Together*, 36.

9. Dane Ortlund, *Deeper: Real Change for Real Sinners* (Wheaton, IL: Crossway, 2021), 111.

10. Louis Berkhof, *Systematic Theology* (Grand Rapids: Eerdmans, 1939), 584.

11. See John Cotton, *The Keyes of the Kingdom of Heaven and Power Thereof According to the Word of God* (1644; repr., Ann Arbor, MI: Text Creation Partnership, 2011), 18, https://quod.lib.umich.edu/e/eebo2/B20727.0001.001/1:3.

12. Charleston Association, "Summary of Church Discipline (1774)," in *Polity: Biblical Arguments on How to Conduct Church Life*, ed. Mark E. Dever (Washington, DC: Center for Church Reform, 2001), 131–33.

13. See Ralph D. Winter, "The Two Structures of God's Redemptive Mission," in *Perspectives on the World Christian Movement, A Reader*, 3rd ed., ed. Ralph D. Winter and Steven C. Hawthorn (Pasadena, CA: William Carey Library, 1999), 220–30.

14. Ed Stetzer identified the explosion of church planting networks as one of the three most important trends that would continue over the next ten years ("3 Important Trends in the Next Ten Years," *Christianity Today*, April 24, 2015, https://churchleaders.com /pastors/pastor-articles/253445-3-important-church-trends-next -10-years.html.

15. Quoted in James H. Kraakevik and Dotsey Welliver, eds., *Partners in the Gospel: The Strategic Role of Partnership in World Evangelization*, Billy Graham Center Monograph series (Wheaton, IL: Billy Graham Center, Wheaton College, 1992), xiii.

16. Tim Keller contrasts movements, which would include networks, with institutions. The four characteristics of a movement, according to Keller, include "vision, sacrifice, flexibility with unity, and spontaneity" (*Center Church: Doing Balanced Gospel-Centered Ministry in Your City* [Grand Rapids: Zondervan, 2012], 339).

17. Keller, *Center Church*, 18; see Richard Lints, *The Fabric of Theology: A Prolegomenon to Evangelical Theology* (Grand Rapids: Eerdmans, 1993), 9.

18. Keller, *Center Church*, 16–17.

19. As Keller writes, "Two churches can have different doctrinal frameworks and ministry expressions but the same theological vision—and they will feel like sister ministries. On the other hand, two churches can have similar doctrinal frameworks and ministry expressions, but different theological visions—and they will feel distinct" (*Center Church*, 21).

20. Neil Powell and John James, *Together for the City: How Collaborative Church Planting Leads to Citywide Movements* (Downers Grove, IL: InterVarsity, 2019), 116–17.

21. Wayne A. Meeks says, "The local groups of Christians not only enjoyed a high level of cohesion and group identity, they also were made aware that they belonged to a larger movement." Meeks later observes, "It is evident, too, that Paul and the other leaders of

the mission worked actively to inculcate the notion of a universal brotherhood of the believers in Jesus. The letters themselves, the messengers who brought them, and the repeated visits to the local assemblies by Paul and his associates all emphasized this interrelatedness" (*The First Urban Christians: The Social World of the Apostles*, 2nd ed. [New Haven, CT: Yale University Press, 2003], 107, 109).

22. Charles A. Wanamaker, *The Epistles to the Thessalonians: A Commentary on the Greek Text* (Grand Rapids: Eerdmans, 1990), 161.

23. Robert Banks writes, "Paul's mission is a grouping of specialists identified by their gifts, backed up by a set of sponsoring families and communities, with a specific function and structure. Its purpose is first the preaching of the gospel and the founding of churches and *then the provision of assistance so that they may reach maturity.* While this clearly involves interrelationship with the local communities, Paul's work is essentially a service organization whose members have personal, not structural, links with the communities and seek to develop rather than eliminate or regulate" (*Paul's Idea of Community: Spirit and Culture in Early House Churches*, 2nd ed. [Grand Rapids: Baker Academic, 2010], 159, emphasis mine)

24. Peter T. O'Brien, *Gospel and Mission in the Writings of Paul: An Exegetical and Theological Analysis* (Grand Rapids: Baker, 1995), 44.

25. See O'Brien, *Gospel and Mission*, 44.

26. See Romans 15:30–32, Ephesians 6:19–20, Colossians 4:2–4; 2 Thessalonians 3:1–2.

27. See Acts 14:27; Ephesians 6:21–22; Colossians 4:7–9

28. See 2 Corinthians 8:16–24; Philippians 2:19–30; Colossians 4:10; 1 Thessalonians 3:2; cf. 3 John 5–8.

29. Acts 11:22–26; 13:1–3; 15:35–36, Romans 16:3–4; 1 Corinthians 16:17–18; Philippians 2:25; Colossians 1:7, 4:12–13, 4:11; Philemon 13. For further study on missional partnerships between local churches and extra-local teams, see J. Hesselgrave, *Planting Churches Cross-Culturally: North and Beyond* (Grand Rapids: Baker Academic, 2000); Banks, *Paul's Idea of Community*, 139–40; Peters,

A Biblical Theology of Missions, 199–242; Luis Bush, "In Pursuit of True Christian Partnership: A Biblical Basis from Philippians," in *Partners in the Gospel.*

30. Dialogue adapted from Frank Capra, dir., *It's a Wonderful Life* (Burbank, CA: Liberty Films, 1946).

31. Peters, *A Biblical Theology of Missions*, 238.

Virtue 2: Gifted Leadership

1. Frank Milton Bristol, *The Life of Chaplain McCabe: Bishop of the Methodist Episcopal Church* (New York: Revell, 1908), 259, https://divinityarchive.com/bitstream/handle/11258/2199/cu319 24008322590.pdf.

2. Bristol, *Life of Chaplain McCabe*, 259.

3. Bristol, *Life of Chaplain McCabe*, 260.

4. While I believe in complementarity, adherence to this view in no way has to downplay the need for gifted women in the church's local and extra-local work. Eckhard Schnabel says, "The circle of Pauline coworkers included a considerable number of women . . . In the list of greetings in his letter to the Romans, Paul mentions the following female coworkers who are now residing in Rome: Phoebe (Rom 16:1–2), Priscilla (Rom 16:3), Mary (Rom 16:6), Junia (Rom 16:7), Tryphaena and Tryphosa (Rom 16:12), and Persis (Rom 16:12). Other women whom Paul's description reveals to be coworkers are Apphia (Philemon 2) and Euodia and Syntyche (Philippians 4:2–3). Their participation in Paul's missionary work is indicated by the Greek affix *syn* ("with"): they have struggled 'with' Paul for the gospel (Phil 4:3). They evidently preached the gospel beside Paul" (*Paul the Missionary: Realities, Strategies, and Methods* [Downers Grove, IL: IVP Academic, 2008], 251).

5. Aubrey Malphurs writes, "A careful reading of Acts reveals that the early church implemented the Great Commission mandate primarily by planting churches. A study of the missionary journeys recorded in Acts reveals that they, in fact, were church planting forays into what was predominantly a pagan culture. As a result of these trips, Paul and others planted high-impact churches in key cities such as Derbe, Lystra, Iconium, Antioch, Philippi, Thessalonica, Berea, Corinth and Ephesus" (*Planting Growing*

Churches for the 21st Century: A Comprehensive Guide for New Churches and Those Desiring Renewal [Grand Rapids: Baker, 2004], 42).

6. O. Palmer Robertson writes, "Nothing in scripture explicitly indicates that the apostolate ever would come to an end. Yet it is generally recognized that no one in the church today functions with the authority of the original apostles" (*The Final Word: A Biblical Response to the Case for Tongues and Prophecy Today* [Edinburgh: Banner of Truth, 1993], 80).

7. D. A. Carson observes, "Paul saw his own apostleship as on a par with that of the Twelve, so far as immediacy of call, witness to the resurrection, grasp of the gospel, and intrinsic authority were concerned" (*Showing the Spirit: A Theological Exposition of 1 Corinthians 12–14* [Grand Rapids: Baker, 1987], 90). Peter T. O'Brien says, "Paul, like Jeremiah, had 'stood in the council of the Lord'; that is, he had received both his gospel and his commission to preach it from the risen and exalted Lord Jesus" (*Gospel and Mission in the Writings of Paul: An Exegetical and Theological Analysis* [Grand Rapids: Baker, 1995], 6).

8. Concerning Ephesians 4:11–13, missiologist Alan Hirsch says this passage is written with a "constitutional weight." Paul uses the aorist indicative in verse 7 ("has been given"), which indicates that the ministry giftings described in verse 11 continue beyond New Testament times through the work of leaders who embody these same ministries (see Hirsch's "Reflections on Movement Dynamics," in *Serving a Movement: Doing Balanced, Gospel-Centered Ministry in Your City*, ed. Timothy Keller [Grand Rapids: Zondervan, 2016], 258).

9. D. A. Carson observes, "Attempts to establish what apostleship means for Paul by simply appealing to the full semantic range of the word as it is found in his writings is deeply flawed at the methodological level" (*Showing the Spirit*, 90).

10. Richard Gaffin writes, "The New Testament uses the Greek word *apostolos* in more than one sense" ("A Cessationist View," in *Are Miraculous Gifts for Today? Four Views*, ed. Wayne Grudem [Grand Rapids: Zondervan, 1996], 45). See 1 Corinthians 4:9 (which seems to include Apollos along with Paul as an apostle),

Galatians 1:19 (where James the Lord's brother is described as
an apostle), 1 Thessalonians 2:6 (where "as apostles of Christ
we" must certainly include Silas and Timothy as indicated by
1 Thessalonians 1:1), Philippians 2:25, and 2 Corinthians 8:23
(where Epaphroditus and Titus are described as apostles of the
churches). Also see Walter Bauer, *A Greek-English Lexicon of the
New Testament*, ed. Frederick William Danker, 3rd ed. (Chicago:
University of Chicago Press, 2000), 122. In the New Testament,
the term *apostolos* can denote a delegate, envoy, or messenger
generally (a *broad* use), the Twelve specifically (a *technical* use:
beyond the norm), or it can appear in ways that apply to Paul or
Ephesian 4 apostolic ministry (a *semi-technical* use). Exegetical
rigor is required, therefore, to discover where *apostle* is being used
as a role that has ceased versus a gift that continues. Here I am
grateful to Jeff Purswell for clarifying these distinctions.

11. Ralph D. Winter, "The Two Structures of God's Redemptive
    Mission," in *Perspectives on the World Christian Movement,
    A Reader*, 3rd ed. (Pasadena, CA: William Carey Library), 222.

12. Vern S. Poythress, "Modern Spiritual Gifts as Analogous to
    Apostolic Gifts: Affirming Extraordinary Works of the Spirit
    within Cessationist Theology," *Journal of the Evangelical
    Theological Society* 39, no. 1 (1996): 71–101, https://frame
    -poythress.org/modern-spiritual-gifts-as-analogous-to-apostolic
    -gifts-affirming-extraordinary-works-of-the-spirit-within
    -cessationist-theology.

13. P. T. O'Brien, *Gospel and Mission in the Writings of Paul* (Grand
    Rapids: Baker, 1993), 55, italics in original.

14. C. H. Spurgeon "All of Grace: A Sermon (No. 3479) Published
    on Thursday, October 7th, 1915, Metropolitan Tabernacle,
    Newington," The Spurgeon Archive, https://archive.spurgeon.org
    /sermons/3479.php.

15. Schnabel, *Paul the Missionary*, 377.

16. Peter O'Brien observes, "Proclaiming the gospel meant for Paul
    not simply an initial preaching or with it the reaping of converts;
    it included also a whole range of nurturing and strengthening
    activities which led to the firm establishment of congregations.
    So, his claim to have 'fulfilled the gospel in an arc right up to

Illyricum' signified that he had established strong churches in strategic centers of this area, such as Thessalonica, Corinth and Ephesus" (*Gospel and Mission*, 43).

17. Gregg R. Allison, *Sojourners and Strangers: The Doctrine of the Church* (Wheaton, IL: Crossway, 2012), 210. Wayne Grudem agrees: "It is noteworthy that no major leader in the history of the church—not Athanasius or Augustine, not Luther or Calvin, not Wesley or Whitefield—has taken to himself the title of 'apostle' or let himself be called an apostle. If any in modern times want to take the title 'apostle' to themselves, they immediately raise the suspicion that they may be motivated by inappropriate pride and desires for self-exaltation, along with excessive ambition and a desire for more authority in the church than any one person should rightfully have" (*Systematic Theology* [Grand Rapids: Zondervan, 1994], 911).

18. George Miley, *Loving the Church, Blessing the Nations: Pursuing the Role of Local Churches in Global Mission* (Downers Grove, IL: InterVarsity, 2003), 51.

19. Keller, "Response to Alan Hirsch," in *Serving a Movement*, 268; compare John Calvin, *Institutes of the Christian Religion* 4.4.2; Poythress, "Modern Spiritual Gifts as Analogous to Apostolic Gifts"; Bruno and Dirks, *Churches Partnering Together*, 66–76.

20. In any movement, apostolically gifted people and organizations serve three critical functions: (1) They act as catalysts; they create and kick-start movements. (2) They inject vision, commitment, and energy into movements at critical junctures to sustain momentum. (3) They play a critical role in the development of leadership, an essential component for the ongoing health and vitality of movements. See Sam Metcalf, *Beyond the Local Church: How Apostolic Movements Can Change the World* (Downers Grove, IL: InterVarsity, 2015), 183.

21. According to D. A. Carson, "Paul saw his own apostleship as on a par with that of the Twelve, so far as immediacy of call, witness to the resurrection, grasp of the gospel, and intrinsic authority were concerned" (*Showing the Spirit: A Theological Exposition of 1 Corinthians 12–14* [Grand Rapids: Baker, 1987], 90).

22. "While this clearly involves interrelationship with the local

communities, Paul's work is essentially a service organization whose members have personal, not structural, links with the communities and seek to develop rather than dominate or regulate" (Robert Banks, *Paul's Idea of Community* [Grand Rapids: Baker Academic, 1994], 169).

23. I'm indebted to Peter Wagner for coining this term that describes what happens when a church feeds on community and has no mission antibodies to fight inward, insular, and self-absorbed community (*Your Church Can Be Healthy* [Nashville: Abingdon, 1979], 79).

24. See Grudem, *Systematic Theology*, 867–69; Edmund Clowney, *The Church* (Downers Grove, IL: InterVarsity; 1995), 65.

25. As George Miley observed, "In most cases, if God's people are to meaningfully participate in God's global mission, they must [first] be affirmed, developed, and released in their ministry gifting right where they live, in the context of the community of believers of which they are a part" (Miley, *Loving the Church, Blessing the Nations*, 51).

26. Peters, *A Biblical Theology of Missions*, 214.

27. New Testament scholar Ernest Best wrote, "Looking at him [Paul] from yet another angle they would have seen him as the chief link between themselves and the other churches he had founded and probably also with that in Antioch. It was through him they heard of other Christians and what they were doing (2 Corinthians 8:1–5) and through him that those other Christians learned of them" (*Paul and His Converts* [New York: T&T Clark, 1988], 25).

28. Robert Banks describes the relationship between extra-local workers and local churches: "The two groups are interdependent and assist one another in their work, but the purpose for which each exists, the skills upon which each depends, and the authority through which each lives are not identical . . . Paul views his missionary operation not as an *ekklesia* but rather as something existing independently alongside the scattered Christian communities. Only in a secondary way does it provide the organizational link between the local churches, suggesting the basis for a wider conception of *ekklesia* of a 'denominational' kind" (*Paul's Idea of Community*, 168–69).

29. *The Rise and Fall of Mars Hill*, Christianity Today podcasts, www.christianitytoday.com/ct/podcasts/rise-and-fall-of-mars-hill.

30. William Shakespeare, *Macbeth*, 3.1.57–60.

31. Thabiti M. Anyabwile, *Finding Faithful Elders and Deacons* (Wheaton, IL: Crossway, 2012), 152.

32. For example, Sam Metcalf says, "Contemporary concepts of accountability and excellence are an invention of modernity, and they can be destructive when applied bluntly to spiritual movements" (*Beyond the Local Church*, 181). I wholeheartedly agree with Metcalf's call not to apply accountability "bluntly," but his first line seems to diminish accountability's importance.

33. Bristol, *Life of Chaplain McCabe*, 260.

Mapping Your Network

1. I'm deeply grateful to Todd Milby, Andy Graham, Doug Paul, and their team at Catapult Church Consulting for helping develop this tool. Any Christian leader would do well to discover more about what they do at www.wearecatapult.org. I believe you'll thank me!

2. Note that the negative and positive numbers used to locate churches on these two continuums are not matters of moral judgment but instead relate to where your church plots on the Network matrix axis below. None of the terms on these charts are intended to have a negative connotation. Rather, they are intended to help us name reality.

3. "What Makes Us Different?" NewThing, accessed July 15, 2022, https://newthing.org.

Virtue 3: Collaboration

1. I'm deeply grateful for the writing and thinking of Simon Sinek, who introduces and unpacks this illustration in his book *The Infinite Game* (New York: Portfolio/Penguin, 2019), 3.

2. Quoted in Bill Hull, *Choose the Life: Exploring a Faith That Embraces Discipleship* (Grand Rapids: Baker, 2004), 107, emphasis added.

3. Quoted in Karim R. Lakhani and Jill A. Panetta, "The Principles of Distributed Innovation," *Innovations* 2, no. 3 (2007), 97.

4. Missiologist David Hesselgrave observes, "Westerners (particularly

North Americans) have a cultural bias toward promoting overindependency on the part of the churches they establish. Even when their churches actually belong to a larger fellowship of churches, the likelihood of those churches assuming an active role in the larger fellowship is not always great" (*Planting Churches Cross-Culturally* [Grand Rapids: Baker Academic, 2000], 300).

5. John R. W. Stott, *The Message of 2 Timothy*, The Bible Speaks Today (Downers Grove, IL: InterVarsity, 1973), 20.
6. See Carl R. Trueman, *The Rise and Triumph of the Modern Self: Cultural Amnesia, Expressive Individualism, and the Road to Sexual Revolution* (Wheaton, IL: Crossway, 2021), 43.
7. See Trueman, *Rise and Triumph*, 44–45.
8. See Trueman, *Rise and Triumph*, 54.
9. I'm grateful to David Brooks and his book *The Second Mountain: The Quest for a Moral Life* (New York: Random House, 2019). His imprint is left on several sections of this chapter.
10. Sebastian Junger, *Tribe: On Homecoming and Belonging* (New York: Twelve, 2016), 47, italics in original.
11. Andy Crouch, *Culture Making: Recovering Our Creative Calling* (Downers Grove, IL: InterVarsity, 2008), 23, adapted from Christian cultural critic Ken Myers.
12. B. B. Warfield, *The Person and Work of Christ* (Philadelphia: Presbyterian & Reformed, 1950), 574.
13. Brooks, *Second Mountain*, 281.

Virtue 4: The Dynamics of Renewal

1. See Washington Irving, *Great American Short Stories* (New York: Fall River, 2016), 12.
2. Martin Luther King Jr., "Remaining Awake Through a Great Revolution," commencement address for Oberlin College in Oberlin, Ohio (June 1965), www2.oberlin.edu/external/EOG/BlackHistoryMonth/MLK/CommAddress.html.
3. Alonzo L. McDonald, "The Grand Inquisitor Lives," in *No God But God: Breaking with the Idols of Our Age*, ed. Os Guinness and John Seel (Chicago: Moody, 1992).
4. See Abraham Kuyper, *Rooted and Grounded: The Church as Organism and Institution* (Grand Rapids: Christian's Library Press, 2013).

5. Brian Sanders, *Underground Church: A Living Example of the Church in Its Most Potent Form* (Grand Rapids: Zondervan/ Exponential, 2018), 64.

6. Timothy Keller, *Center Church: Doing Balanced, Gospel-Centered Ministry in Your City* (Grand Rapids: Zondervan, 2012), 338.

7. Roland Allen, *The Spontaneous Expansion of the Church* (Grand Rapids: Eerdmans, 1962), 99.

8. Bono and the Edge, "Stuck in a Moment You Can't Get Out Of," track 2 on *All That You Can't Leave Behind* (Dublin: HQ, 2001).

9. See Underhill's actual quote in Elisabeth Elliot, *On Asking God Why: Reflections on Trusting God* (Grand Rapids: Revell, 2006), 147: "If God were small enough to be understood, he would not be big enough to be worshiped."

10. Richard F. Lovelace, *Dynamics of Spiritual Life: An Evangelical Theology of Renewal* (Downers Grove, IL: IVP Academic, 1979), 65.

11. Lovelace, *Dynamics of Spiritual Life*, 72.

12. Charles Spurgeon, "Christ and His Co-Workers," a sermon preached at the Metropolitan Tabernacle, June 10, 1886, The Spurgeon Center, www.spurgeon.org/resource-library/sermons/ christ-and-his-co-workers.

13. Douglas J. Moo, *The Epistle to the Romans*, New International Commentary on the New Testament (Grand Rapids: Eerdmans, 1996), 896.

14. Quoted in John Piper, "Soundbites from the Battlefield," *Desiring God*, November 25, 1991, www.desiringgod.org/articles/sound bites-from-the-battlefield.

15. Donald Hagner writes, "After the initial statement concerning Jesus' authority, which has the parallelism *en ouranw kai epi [tees] gees*—'in heaven and on [the] earth (v. 18b)'—the commission proper consists syntactically of the main verb *matheeteusate*— 'make disciples'—with three parallel subordinate participles: *poreuthentes*, 'going,' *baptizontes*, 'baptizing,' and *didaskontes*, 'teaching' (vv. 19–20a). The participles when linked with the imperative verb themselves take on imperatival force and function as imperatives" (*Matthew 14–28*, Word Biblical Commentary, vol. 33b [Dallas, TX: Word, 1995], 882).

16. Robert Coleman observed, "The Great Commission of Christ

given to his Church summed it up in the command to 'make disciples of every creature' (Matt. 28:19). The word here indicates that the disciples were to go out into the world and win others who would come to be what they themselves were—disciples of Christ. This mission is emphasized even more when the Greek text of the passage is studied, and it is seen that the words *go, baptize,* and *teach* are all participles that derive their force from the one controlling verb 'make disciples.' This means that the Great Commission is not merely to go to the ends of the earth preaching the gospel (Mark 16:15), nor to baptize a lot of converts into the name of the triune God, nor to teach them the precepts of Christ, but to 'make disciples'–to build men like themselves who were so constrained by the commission of Christ that they not only followed his way but led others to as well. Only as disciples were made could the other activities of the commission fulfill their purpose" (Robert E. Coleman, *The Master Plan of Evangelism* [1964; repr., Grand Rapids: Revell, 2010], 104).

Virtue 5: A Kingdom Mindset

1. Oscar Cullmann, *Christ and Time: The Primitive Christian Conception of Time and History,* 3rd ed., trans. Floyd V. Filson (1950; repr., Eugene, OR: Wipf & Stock, 2018), 146.
2. George Eldon Ladd, *A Theology of the New Testament,* rev. ed. (Grand Rapids: Eerdmans, 1993), 67.
3. R. C. Sproul, "What Is the Kingdom of God?" Ligonier Ministries, September 13, 2021, www.ligonier.org/learn/articles/what-is-king dom-god.
4. Dane Ortlund, *Gentle and Lowly: The Heart of Christ for Sinners and Sufferers* (Wheaton, IL: Crossway, 2020), 192–93.
5. The concept of covenant appears in the organizing documents of the Charleston Association, a Baptist network founded in 1751: "It appears advisable that these delegates, at their first meeting, *should in a formal manner enter into covenant with each other* (emphasis mine), as the representatives of the churches, for the promoting of Christ's cause in general and for the interest of the churches they represent in particular" (in *Polity: Biblical Arguments for How to Conduct Church Life, A Collection of*

Historic Baptist Documents, ed. Mark E. Dever [Washington, DC: Center for Church Reform, 2001], 131.

6. Paul E. Miller, *A Loving Life: In a World of Broken Relationships* (Wheaton, IL: Crossway, 2014), 24.

7. Winn Collier, *A Burning in My Bones: The Authorized Biography of Eugene H. Peterson* (Colorado Springs: WaterBrook, 2021), 129, italics in original.

8. Isaac Adams, *Talking about Race: Gospel Hope for Hard Conversations* (Grand Rapids: Zondervan, 2022), 143.

Virtue 6: Humility

1. David McCullough, *John Adams* (New York: Simon & Schuster, 2001), 421.

2. Timothy Dwight, "Sermon XXVII: On the Love of Distinction," in *Sermons*, vol. 1 (Edinburgh: Waugh & Innes, 1828), 523–24.

3. James L. Swanson, *Manhunt: The 12-Day Chase for Lincoln's Killer* (New York: HarperCollins, 2006), 205.

4. Walter Isaacson, *Steve Jobs: The Exclusive Biography* (New York: Simon & Schuster, 2011), 119.

5. Dave Harvey, *The Plurality Principle: How to Build and Maintain a Thriving Church Leadership Team* (Wheaton, IL: Crossway, 2021), 75.

6. Scott M. Manetsch, *Calvin's Company of Pastors: Pastoral Care and the Emerging Reformed Church, 1536–1609*, Oxford Studies in Historical Theology (New York: Oxford University Press, 2013), 63.

7. Dietrich Bonhoeffer, *Life Together: A Discussion of Christian Fellowship* (San Francisco: Harper & Row, 1954), 109.

8. John Chrysostom, *On the Priesthood* 5.4, trans. Graham Neville (New York: St Vladimir's Seminary, 1996), 130.

9. C. S. Lewis, *Mere Christianity* (1943; repr., New York: Macmillan, 1960), 114, italics in original.

10. See Rick Warren, *The Purpose Driven Life: What on Earth Am I Here For?* (2002; repr., Grand Rapids: Zondervan, 2012), 149; Timothy Keller, *The Freedom of Self-Forgetfulness: The Path to True Christian Joy* (Leyland, UK: 10Publishing, 2012).

11. Dave Harvey, *Rescuing Ambition* (Wheaton, IL: Crossway, 2010).

12. Alexis de Tocqueville, *Democracy in America* (New York: Perennial Classics, 2000), 632.

Virtue 7: Modesty

1. "Mycorrhizas," Trees for Life, accessed July 20, 2022, https:// treesforlife.org.uk/into-the-forest/habitats-and-ecology/ecology /mycorrhizas.
2. Ferris Jabr, "The Social Life of Forests," *New York Times Magazine*, December 2, 2020, www.nytimes.com/interactive /2020/12/02/magazine/tree-communication-mycorrhiza.html. Jabr writes, "By analyzing the DNA in root tips and tracing the movement of molecules through underground conduits, [the researcher Suzanne] Simard has discovered that fungal threads link nearly every tree in a forest—even trees of different species. Carbon, water, nutrients, alarm signals and hormones can pass from tree to tree through these subterranean circuits. Resources tend to flow from the oldest and biggest trees to the youngest and smallest. Chemical alarm signals generated by one tree prepare nearby trees for danger. Seedlings severed from the forest's underground lifelines are much more likely to die than their networked counterparts. And if a tree is on the brink of death, it sometimes bequeaths a substantial share of its carbon to its neighbors."
3. See Olivia Box, "What Happens to a Tree When It Dies," *JSTOR Daily*, March 31, 2021, https://daily.jstor.org/what-happens-to-a -tree-when-it-dies.
4. Matthew Sleeth, *Reforesting Faith: What Trees Teach Us about the Nature of God and His Love for Us* (Colorado Springs: WaterBrook, 2019), 102.
5. G. K. Chesterton, *Orthodoxy* (1908; repr., New York: Dover, 2020), 23.
6. Steve Earl, "Haven't You Been Good," track 1 on *I Stand in Awe*, © 1998 Sovereign Grace Worship, https://sovereigngracemusic.org /music/songs/havent-you-been-good.
7. C. S. Lewis, *Surprised by Joy: The Shape of My Early Life* (1955; repr., New York: Harcourt, Brace, Jovanovich, 1966), 207.
8. I'm deeply grateful for Clint Clifton, dear friend and one of the

sharpest church planting gurus I know, for the conversations in which his ideas on church life cycles shaped and sharpened my own thinking.

9. Albert Mohler, "Podcast: Mohler on Why Young Christians Should Prioritize Institutions," *TGC Podcast*, November 20, 2020, www.thegospelcoalition.org/podcasts/tgc-podcast/mohler-young-christians-prioritize-institutions.

10. John Calvin, *Institutes of the Christian Religion*, ed. John T. McNeill; trans. Ford Lewis Battles (Philadelphia: Westminster, 2001), 1:714.

11. Years ago, I read Alonzo McDonald's words about the idol of immortality for Christian organizations ("The Grand Inquisitor Lives," in *No God But God: Breaking with the Idols of our Age*, ed. Os Guinness and John Seel (Chicago: Moody, 1992), chapter 7. I'm grateful for being introduced to that idea through his chapter and for the staying power of this concept over the years.

12. Lin-Manuel Miranda, Twitter post, February 24, 2015, 10:09 a.m., https://twitter.com/lin_manuel/status/570239151666270208.

13. J. I. Packer, *A Quest for Godliness: The Puritan Vision of the Christian Life* (Wheaton, IL: Crossway, 1990), 118.

GREAT COMMISSION COLLECTIVE

PLANTING CHURCHES.
STRENGTHENING LEADERS.

Great Commission Collective partners churches together to see churches multiplied. We believe that healthy churches spring from healthy leaders, and so we intentionally invest time and resources into helping leaders last. We also seek to strengthen elder pluralities so they can develop and lead healthy churches. We believe that the more churches thrive under healthy leaders, the more they will multiply.

The collective seeks to plant churches and strengthen leaders through a culture marked by Gospel Integrity, Relational Connection, Intentional Care, Deliberate Collaboration, Contextual Application, Healthy Plurality, and Kingdom Focus.

For more information on the Great Commission Collective, visit https://gccollective.org or email info@gccollective.org.

REV DAVE HARVEY

Dave Harvey has spent years developing marriage, leadership, and gospel-centered material and has traveled nationally and abroad to teach how the gospel transforms lives. Many of Dave's insights, teachings, and free resources in areas of leadership, preaching, marriage, and plurality have been collected on his website at https://revdaveharvey.com.

Dave is the author of *When Sinners Say I Do*, *Am I Called?*, *Rescuing Ambition*, *Letting Go: Rugged Love for Wayward Souls* (coauthored with Paul Gilbert), *I Still Do! Growing Closer and Stronger through Life's Defining Moments*, *The Plurality Principle*, and *Stronger Together: Seven Partnership Virtues and the Vices That Subvert Them*.

For more information on Dave's books, visit https://revdaveharvey.com/books